Marketing, Managing and Contact Lenses

□ □ □
□ □ □
□ □ □

Marketing, Managing and Contact Lenses

Robert A. Koetting, O.D., F.A.A.O.

With a contribution by

William E. Fleischman, M.S., O.D., F.A.A.O.

250101

Butterworth-Heinemann

Boston London Oxford Singapore Sydney Toronto Wellington

Library of Congress Cataloging-in-Publication Data

Koetting, Robert A.
    Marketing, managing and contact lenses / R.A. Koetting : with a
contribution by William E. Fleischman.
        p.   cm.
    Includes bibliographical references.
    ISBN 0-7506-9175-1
    1. Contact lenses.   2. Optometry—Practice.   3. Optometry—
Marketing.   I. Title.
    [DNLM: 1. Contact lenses.   2. Marketing of Health Services.
3. Practice Management, Medical.   WW 355 K784m]
RE977.C6K65   1992
617.7'523'068—dc20
DNLM/DLC
for Library of Congress   91-43242
                                                                          CIP

British Library Cataloguing in Publication Data

Koetting, Robert A.
    Marketing, managing and contact lenses.
    I. Title
    617.7523

    ISBN 0-7506-9175-1

Butterworth-Heinemann
80 Montvale Avenue
Stoneham, MA 02180

10   9   8   7   6   5   4   3   2   1

Printed in the United States of America

*Dedicated to the man who made me study optometry
when I really wanted to be an engineer:*

Felix A. Koetting, O.D., D.O.S., F.A.A.O.
1893–1983

□ □ □
□ □ □
□ □ □

Contents

☐ ☐ ☐
☐ ☐ ☐
☐ ☐ ☐

Foreword

At last, here is a book written by an eminently successful contact lens clinician who is also a marketing and practice management expert.

The contemporary optometrist must combine superior professional skills with the outlook of a chief executive officer of a corporation to achieve success in practice. Incorporating Dr. Koetting's suggestions into an established practice will improve the overall success of the practice. For the newly established optometrist, using this book as a guide can place their practice on a firm footing.

I have known and worked with Dr. Koetting on various projects for more than 20 years. I am grateful that he was able to crystallize his thoughts and clearly record his techniques for professional success and community recognition.

Paul Farkas, M.S., O.D., F.A.A.O.
Diplomate Contact Lens Section—American Academy of Optometry
Adjunct Professor of Optometric Economics
Southeastern University of the Health Sciences
College of Optometry
North Miami Beach, Florida

Preface

Professional authors may just sit down and grind out volumes, but this writer is certainly not one of them. When I retired from practice in 1985, it seemed that every well-wisher ended our conversation with, "You'll have to write a book," a directive that couldn't have sounded more unlikely at the time.

Then, given some idle moments to reflect on the matter, it became increasingly obvious that most old-timers have slipped out of fashion, and simultaneously out of print. So who would want to see a book about contact lenses that doesn't even discuss polymegathism or boundary effects? Some students, technicians, and practitioners, hopefully, but mostly, I would! I really want to share 30 years' practical experience with those who aspire to learn the art and science.

By a happy twist of fate, I was there in 1957 when Newton Wesley and George Jessen popularized the idea that savvy practitioners (with a little laboratory cooperation) could succeed in our highly specialized field. We felt good about ourselves, worked closely with manufacturers, honed skills, and fitted lenses to an ever-expanding number of patients. It was a wonderful era. If Horatio Alger had lived in the twentieth century, he'd most likely have been making contact lenses.

By 1971 many of the comfort problems had been eliminated, and millions of additional patients were wearing them. When hydrogels entered the picture, so did "big business"—out went the pioneers and the garrett inventors.

The changes weren't all bad at first. The Food and Drug Administration (FDA) approved tints, and the introduction of extended-wear lenses eliminated handling fears for many people. Soft bifocals were approved in 1982, and the "golden age" arrived. Fees remained high enough to make contact lens–fitting procedures attractive, but enthusiasm dipped as professionals began to think that "anyone can do it."

Later, when extended-wear Rigid Gas Permeable Lenses (RGP) came along, another dangerous trend became obvious: if any design could be worn successfully by a given number of people, fitting techniques seemed virtually insignificant. In many quarters, "approval" became synonymous with "successful."

By the time disposables were introduced, a race to see who could manufacture the greatest number at the lowest per unit cost began in earnest. Computer-driven research placed emphasis on the percentage of people who could wear any given size or shape. Production of contact lenses has now reached an all time high, regulated by a series of "80-20" rules: Manufacturers seem satisfied if any given lens fits 80% of the patients, and doctors appear equally satisfied if 80% of the people entering their offices leave without asking for a refund. A giant mediocrity exists. The majority is satisfied with the statistics, while hard-to-fit patients wind up with glasses.

Furthermore, because contact lens–fitting procedures have been so simplified, there is little perceived difference between the highly skilled practitioner and the amateur clinician. Without distinguishing characteristics between the two, price has often become the common denominator, and fees drop accordingly—hence, a strong motivation to fit spectacles or to perform other more lucrative services. For doctors who possess special talents, the obvious solution is a practice dedicated to problem cases and specialty lens-fitting. It's not that simple, you say? You're right, there *is* more to it!

I've called this book *Marketing, Managing and Contact Lenses*. Successful practice involves all three, and that is what this book is all about.

□ □ □
□ □ □
□ □ □

Market Pearls

Collecting ideas in succinct orderly groups has considerable appeal, as evidenced by David Wallechinsky and the Wallaces who penned two best-selling books by simply compiling lists with neither a plot nor thread of continuity. There are lists in this book, too, covering quite a variety of subjects. Marketing and managing pearls are assembled for your reference (indicated by □ □ □ □ □), but for your needs they may be inconveniently scattered throughout the text. To simplify the search to review specific topics, you will find them as follows:

Chapter 9

Chapter 10

Chapter 11

Chapter 12

Chapter 13

Chapter 14

Marketing, Managing and Contact Lenses

1

□ □ □
□ □ □
□ □ □

Goal-Setting

I want to get you fired up right now. First of all, because you won't read the rest of this book if you're not, but mostly because it's good for you!

"Don't pull that Tom Peters, Zig Ziglar stuff on me," you say, "my practice is different." OK, let's not argue. Stick with me and maybe you will change your mind.

Let's start by agreeing that everyone needs to get organized. I don't know where I borrowed the idea, but I've repeated it in lectures for so many years you may as well take my word for it. There are three essential steps that every optometrist detests. They hate to

1. think
2. follow an orderly procedure
3. write anything down

Concentrate on *thinking* for the moment. You do it in the shower, when you are waiting for stoplights, airplanes, or your next patient. If you really can't take time for some serious introspection, try making an annual retreat. Considered a religious exercise for many years, the idea is now catching on without noticeable spiritual significance. There are a growing number of places offering you an opportunity to set aside a day or two in silence to consider your objectives. Personally, I've found this form of meditation more valuable and productive than any other approach to facing the future.

On that same subject, don't overlook the possibility of a good career counselor. Only a few hours of assistance each month may keep you on track. Some achievers might view using professional help as a weakness. If that's your problem, remember that you are doing everything on your own. A counselor simply helps you do it better. If you decide you need such help, talk with several. Ask about their training, experience, specialties, and fee payment arrangements. If you aren't comfortable with one individual, forget it. After all, your practice is at stake.

Your Practice Isn't Really Different

Now let's get back to those similarities. We might call them the seven deadly sins of optometric practice in general and contact lens practice in particular.

□ □ □ □ □ The Seven Deadly Sins of Practice Management

1. believing your practice is *different*
2. failure to identify the competition
3. believing that good doctors don't have to advertise
4. buying cheap materials to improve the net
5. ·overestimating the stability of your practice
6. believing that doing it yourself produces better results
7. looking for greener pastures

My Practice Is Different

I may be sharing a secret with you, but if you've done any lecturing, you already know that voices carry very well in a hushed room. Somehow audiences feel they can see and hear a speaker but are not personally discernable from the podium. Even though I have often wished that were true, I've heard some skeptical remarks from time to time, and for the most part, they are in essence saying, "That won't work in my practice."

"He's from the city," says the rural practitioner. "That's OK for the Midwest," states the New Yorker, and the fellow in the next block with no geographic distinction mutters, "He probably kicks back to ophthalmologists." Most of us really want to be unique.

You've probably already figured out that my comments here easily relate to suburban specialized practice, so you're expecting they won't apply to the inner city or health centers or franchises or small town main street. Not so!

We didn't call them ghettos then, but my first office neighborhood was only distinguished by the use of old-fashioned chalk instead of today's spray-painted graffiti. I've practiced in a medical office, a small town, and a discount house. More than a half century ago, I entered our field checking lenses in a "wholesale" lab, so there isn't much I haven't tried.

Take my word for it: the more you may think you are different, the more we are the same. Sure, it takes longer in the city. You certainly have to plan ahead when you're salaried, no doubt about it. Please don't let that stand in the way.

Look at the concept without being specific. "Class" in your office might not be a Rembrandt or a Picasso, but if the things you do show more taste than your neighborhood requires, you will appeal to people who are willing to spend a little more to get the best. Gleaning something useful from the experience of others, without automatically saying "I am different," is a challenge we all face.

Identifying the Competition

Mighty nations compete for space on earth, and tiny cells compete for oxygen. Price houses are as unobtrusive as fire trucks. No identification problem there, but is that really your competition?

Our competitors literally include everyone from the guy across the street to a sweatshop in Korea, and failure to place them in proper perspective can result in serious misuse of productive efforts—challenging windmills.

If You Are	*You May Think Your Competition Is*
A small town doctor	Big practices in a big city
A big city practitioner	Price houses and large chains
Working for a chain	An even bigger chain or cheaper price house
A chain owner	Some foreign conglomerate
A small independent practitioner	A Health Maintenance Organization (HMO) with a captive patient base
Working for an HMO	A small independent practitioner offering personalized service and having the freedom to provide any form of care
A typical O.D.	Some M.D.
A typical M.D.	Some O.D.

But Is It?

Competition is just about anything that keeps a patient out of your office. It might be money spent on video equipment, an automobile, or a ski trip. If some persuasive individual goes to another optometrist and refers friends to that office, does the patient or the doctor represent competition? Once we bow to the influence of things other people do, we've lost control. As Pogo has been saying for years, "We has met the enemy and it is us." In one way or another, everything is competition. Learn to say "So what!"

We won't dwell on statistics here, but things certainly aren't as bad as some might think. There is no reason to believe that optometric income has not at least kept pace with inflation. The future of the profession can best be judged by the number of individual patients it serves, and that number continues to increase. In a recent survey, 86% of the American Optometric Association (AOA) members responding were self-employed (American Optometric Association, 1991). In the same survey, 47% did not believe that the percentage of patients taking prescriptions elsewhere was increasing. More eye examinations are being performed and patients seek this service more often. Although 32% of the examinations are, at least partly, covered by insurance, the result has been an increased awareness of the need for vision care. The prospects are anything but bleak, and you are in control.

Doctors Advertise

Our second misconception dealt with the idea that good doctors don't have to advertise. Nothing could be further from the truth. When Leo Durocher said, "Nice guys finish last," he could easily have addressed those words to we independent practitioners. Hospitals advertise, insurance companies advertise, HMOs advertise, large medical practices advertise, articles planted in newspapers by public relations firms are a common and effective form of advertising, etc., etc. We will deal with this in greater depth later.

Buy Cheap, Sell Cheap?

"What would you charge if contact lenses were free?" Irv Bennett used to ask. No prudent practitioner would spend an exorbitant amount for materials. Overpaying is in the best interest of neither the patient nor the practice, but the price of lenses has been a scapegoat long enough. Of course, large chains buy lenses for a dollar or two less (while meeting unbelievably high overhead costs), but most of them would gladly pay the higher price if they could be assured of *your* net percentage per patient.

This is mostly a contact lens book so we'll disregard frame and fashion tints for the moment, but the same principles apply. The professional sells service. The vast differences that exist in contact lens charges is certainly not justified by the relatively small difference in the price of competitive lenses.

Paying too much for a thing does not ensure quality, buy paying too little may be taking a chance on the alternative. Any optometrist who is barely surviving while charging $200 for a pair of contact lenses is not losing patients to the $39.50 price house because the chain is paying $4 less for materials.

The Stable Practice

Hardly anyone knows a fully retired optometrist. The majority seems to putter along on a part-time basis years past the age when those in any other field should be confined to a lawn chair. Having no definite retirement plan is just the tip of the iceberg.

This idea that life will go on forever unchanged contributes to complacency which prevents really aggressive practice building and reinforces the groundless faith that patient loyalty will maintain a dollar volume ad infinitum. Patients are only loyal up to a point, of course, and this lack of dependability contributes to another area of serious disappointment.

When an O.D. takes in a recent graduate, the established optometrist is very likely living up to the practice's potential, yet blissfully assuming that the same number of faithful patients will somehow cover this added expense. The $40,000 or $50,000 actually represents a genuine reduction in the senior doctor's take-home income. The new practitioner must generate enough gross to net an equal amount before the established practitioner can break even. It is certainly not an impossible risk; hundreds take it every year with mostly pleasant consequences. Many more have, unfortunately, gone down the road to a bitter parting because the practice just could not support another professional without substantial change.

Senior doctors tend to be resistant, recognizing that new procedures may be theoretically and academically appropriate, but somehow certain that a mode of operation that has worked for 20 or 30 years can't be all bad. Never overestimate the stability of a practice.

Do It Yourself

We'll talk about this matter in substantial detail later on. Possibly borne of insecurity and fathered by ego, most professionals—optometrists are certainly not alone here—work under the burden of a nagging complex that screams, "If you want a job done right, do it yourself." This is sometimes paraphrased, "If you want a job done cheap, etc." The reasons may vary, but the whole problem is characterized by an ever-present fear that releasing even the slightest amount of authority will lead to disaster.

We all know colleagues who believe that new associates should earn their keep even though most patients don't want to see the new doctor. They assume quite rightly that the new practitioner will make a good many mistakes so that both will have some difficulty achieving financial success. Still, there is little likelihood that any of us will not grow older. The inevitable must be faced.

Is the Grass Really Greener?

Our most precious asset is what we already know. The most valuable patients are the ones we already have. The easiest practice to develop is the one we have right now, and what's more, it will cost a lot less.

What percentage of our lives have we spent in optometry? Can we really justify disregarding it to enter another field? So why dabble in a car wash, a fast-food franchise, diving for treasure, or trying the commodities market? Time and money invested anywhere else cannot produce a return equal to the results of that same effort put into the thing that we all know best.

There is no such thing as a free lunch. When you are not thinking about your practice, you are thinking about something else, and the good ideas that might have been will never see the light of day. How much is your time worth? Develop a perspective.

When you are not personally involved in management or promotional activities, either nothing is happening or you have hired someone to carry on. Let's assume you are paying that person. How much could you really save, instead of hiring someone else, while you are

- washing your car, cutting the grass, or painting your house?
- babysitting so your spouse could pursue a career that is in no way related to the practice?
- shopping for bargains and traveling long distances to buy discounted shoes, suits, or furniture?
- driving an extra twenty minutes each way (more than 3 weeks annually) because homes in your neighborhood sell for a little less?
- reading the stock market report so you can learn enough to make a killing in some field about which you know little or nothing?
- "moonlighting" at the expense of being available during convenient hours in your own office?

It is indeed a matter of attitude. The person who is dedicated to success in any field, and in this case we are talking about contact lens practice, will make that a first priority when it comes to time, money, and enthusiasm. There is no blueprint for success, and none is needed. The grass is greener right here at home.

When Times Get Tough

Napoleon Hill said that success or failure is much more a matter of mental attitude than mental capacity, and we are in real trouble if he was right (Hill 1987). A ubiquitous pessimism seems to hang over the contact lens field. Pessimism is *in* despite the facts.

America has the world's greatest concentration of multiple wage-earners in families. One member laid off is not tantamount to destruction. On the contrary, one less worker may provide additional leisure activity and is frequently welcomed—more meals with the family, camp outs, gardening, do-it-yourself projects, etc. A study once involved asking a thousand persons how much it cost to buy what one dollar might a year before. The average estimate was nearly seven times the actual increase in the consumer price index. People have always worried about their pocketbooks, but usually they have considered this a personal issue and have picked other things—the Middle East, civil rights, crime—as more important public issues. With some of these fears behind us, the majority appears to soak in only bad news, so let's take a look at the other side of the coin.

From an objective nonconsumer point of view, the outlook is a good deal brighter. During inflationary periods, as during a recession, people buy because they fear they will not have money later on. Consumers want to use their cash while it will still buy something. The more they talk poor, the more they spend rich.

This is especially so among younger patients, who are by no means stereotyped. Those in school and living at home have a good deal of discretionary money. Many new homemakers are not as impressed with opulent appliances as their parents were at the same age. They still buy luxuries, but of a different kind. During the 1960s, cartoonist Al Capp once had a character say, "This must be a very rich neighborhood, look how badly the children are dressed!" Characteristically, people like to play at being something they are not.

A couple of years ago, the movie *Pretty Woman* was a box office smash without a justifiable plot. Viewers simply wanted to share the fantasy of unattainable extravagance, as they did much earlier when *The Great Gatsby* revived a look of "elegance" that characterized a segment of the population during the depression a generation before. When people don't have money, the appearance of wealth becomes important. Luxuries, like designer frames or cosmetic lenses, mean much more to those who have less to spend. In any sagging economy, some O.D.s will be too busy to handle the volume, while others wring their hands in despair. Instead of looking at unemployment percentages, efforts can be better directed to those who still work, make money, and spend it on the things they want.

Success begins with an open mind. Most practices are not *really* different. Now that we have that out of the way, let's go on!

Are You a Small Business Owner?

The business of professional practice is very much a *business*. In 1989, accountants Anders, Minkler, and Diehl reported on 3000 companies that began operations 3 years previous. Here are the characteristics about these entrepreneurs:

□ □ □ □ □ Characteristics of Successful Small Business Owners

- They work *long,* but not *excessive* hours. Some 80% of those who worked 60–69 hours per week were still in business at the end of the 3 years. The survival rate was far lower for those who worked fewer hours.
- They devote *full time* to business. Dissipating their time and energy with a second job reduced their chances of success.
- They emphasize *service over price.* The survival rate was 82% for those that did versus 70% for those who relied on low price.
- They are *self-confident.* The self-assured were more likely to survive during the first 3 years of business.
- They *know their product/service.* Those who had worked with the same product or service in prior jobs showed an 80% survival rate versus 70% for those who hadn't.
- They *secure substantial capital investment.* Those starting their companies with investments exceeding $50,000 had a 10% better success rate than those who started with less than $20,000.

Some Words for Those Under 40

If your hair is as gray as mine, you can skip this part, but if you think that 40 is a long way off, beware—everybody who is 40, 50, and beyond once thought the same.

But, take heart. If you are doing the right things now, the odds are they'll pay off after that "watershed" birthday. Despite the widespread assumption that work gets harder after 40 (and of course some things like remembering patients' names or getting up without stiff knees really do), familiarity with your practice makes work dramatically easier. Responsibilities are heavier, but your know-how and judgment compensate for extra hours of work. In big businesses as well, the Lear jets, limosines, and decorator-designed offices seldom go to people under 40 who are still doing the actual work. "Golden parachutes" are there only for those who have risen high enough to strap one on.

I read once that after 40 most successful people are simply finding better ways to use what they already know. After 40, it's judgment, a sense of how to manage people, and a sensible set of goals that matter in most jobs. Lawyers, for example, learn the law in their 20s. In their 30s, they learn the legal profession (not the same thing as the law at all). After 40, they put what they know to use. It is the same in eyecare.

We're talking about goal setting and planning here. After 40, you should be recognizable as a complete person with your own special style. You can experiment in your 20s and 30s, but by the time you are 40, nothing looks more insecure than trying to redesign your looks in mid-career. By the time you've reached middle age, you'd better know what you're good at, what you enjoy doing, and what you do better than anyone else.

If you haven't established a network of friends, or at least people who are obligated to you for one reason or another, by the time you are 40, you're in trouble. It's never too late, but a network is not something you can establish overnight. It's the result of working on it for decades. In business and politics, you need a lot of people, spread out in the right places, who you can rely on when the moment comes—even if it's for no more than saying a few good things about you at a party.

A One-Sentence Goal

The Nightengale Connection

On March 25, 1989, at age 68, Earl Nightengale died in Scottsdale, Arizona, after a full and most unusual life. Almost miraculously, he was 1 of only 12 who survived the December 7 attack on the *Arizona* at Pearl Harbor. He went into radio in Chicago, working 18 hours a day, six and seven days a week, for 7 years (and if you are old enough to remember, during four of those years he was also the voice of "Sky King" on the radio series).

With enviable wealth at the age of 35, Nightengale quit broadcasting to develop a series of recorded motivational messages. Long before cassettes, he collaborated with Lloyd Conant in a series called *Lead The Field* (Nightengale 1961). That was in 1961, and contact lenses held a lot of promise, but like many other O.D.s, I had my doubts. His record literally changed my life!

Unfortunately, I never met the man. Once, toward the end of his career, I heard him speak, but regretfully, didn't even shake his hand nor share with him the profound impression his philosophy made on my life.

"Sum up your goal in one sentence," Nightengale said. All other objectives are really just steps toward reaching it. For example:

Goal: To have the biggest specialty contact lens practice in my state.

☐ ☐ ☐ ☐ ☐ Realistic Steps Toward Achieving Your Goal

Sixty percent patient annual referral rate

- Determine present referral rate and check semiannually
- Increase referrals to at least .3 per active patient per year
- Send thank you notes
- Send flowers to persons who refer three people
- Tell everyone in the office you are still accepting difficult cases
- Remind parents to bring in children
- Etc.

Fifteen percent referrals from personal contacts

- Join neighborhood associations
- Become active in Rotary
- Accept presidency of PTA
- Volunteer for assignments at church
- Etc.

Ten percent referrals from other optometrists

- Attend all local and state society meetings
- Volunteer to head state contact lens committee
- Write a contact lens–related article for the state journal in March and September
- Volunteer for local society program in June, and repeat annually
- Etc.

Ten percent new patient referrals from ophthalmologists

- Identify and establish mailing lists
- Call on (or have lunch with) one ophthalmologist each week
- Send reports on all new patients
- Develop a short newsletter to be mailed quarterly
- Refer patients on a rotational basis
- Etc.

Five percent referrals from staff

- Discuss at meeting each month
- Give TV to person bringing in most personal friends by October

- Send group to paraoptometric meeting in April
- Etc.

Other steps towards achieving this goal might be purely personal. They might involve investing in a better location, equipment, or clinical expertise.

Improve your skills

- Attend regional congress in February
- Attend Vision Expo in September
- Read contact lens journal and complete quizzes each month
- Etc.

Nightengale talked about a rudderless ship, constantly moving but never getting anywhere. So many of our colleagues still seem to have that problem. Those O.D.s who sound most discouraged at meetings usually like to boast about their investments and their many other activities, time spent in pursuits that add nothing to practice development.

Write your goal on a slip of paper, he said, put a sign on the bathroom mirror or paste it to your telephone. Debate every issue by asking, "Will this help to meet my objective?" Sure it's a corny idea, but it worked.

Heeding this advice, I bought equipment, hired personnel, talked about and planned for a practice that was not to be for quite a while. Sure, I made some mistakes and paid for every one of them. The most serious probably involved delaying the move into a better location. Higher rent, I found, is almost always a good investment.

You Are Who You Are

Nightengale began with the premise that you are who you are, and his philosophy guided me through a healthy process of communication with patients, colleagues, and friends. "What should I do about my diabetes, or cataracts, hearing loss, or athlete's foot?" "See your own doctor," I would reply, "my specialty is contact lenses." I think people really respected the fact that I didn't try to know everything. Being good in only one field was no disgrace; it actually proved to be a tremendous asset. Furthermore, such candor relieves a lot of stress. An old Chinese proverb implies that one cannot be truly content until one learns to say, "I don't know."

Invest in Yourself

From some other source, Nightengale told the story of a man who bought a stove and sat down before the cold metal box. If this thing works, he promised himself, I am going to buy some coal for it — like the same foolish rationale that has been the ruination of countless practices.

Applied to optometry there are at least ten things that should not be put off until the practice volume "justifies" the investment.

☐ ☐ ☐ ☐ ☐ Investments that Can't Be Put Off

1. the right location for your type of practice
2. a competent staff
3. networking at professional meetings (see Chapter 14)
4. promotional activity
5. high-tech instrumentation
6. a large inventory
7. quality printed materials
8. attractive furnishings
9. twenty-four-hour telephone coverage
10. a computer with the proper software

You may remember Earl Nightengale's "Acres of Diamonds" story. It probably wasn't new with him, but that's not important.

A disparing farmer, discouraged after years of trying to make crops grow in the stubborn black soil, spent years traveling around the world looking for greener pastures. Finally, at the end of his wasted life, he returned to discover that the ugly black sand was you-know-what, and he had literally been sitting on acres of diamonds.

Nightengale didn't waste much time getting to the moral, and he was absolutely right. Get good at what you do!

The Magic Word Is "Attitude"

From that day when I first heard the "Magic Word" until I retired 25 years later, I was confident of success. Not outstanding by some standards perhaps, but more than enough to give its source credit for the common sense advice that every activity should be *goal*-oriented. People without a sense of direction are like ships without rudders. Self-confidence comes from recognizing that goal, you are what you *think* you are. Failure to plan for success is like expecting heat from an "empty stove." Don't worry about the other guy. *Just be sure of yourself.*

A Sense of Direction

Let's face it, for the most part new graduates are bewildered. Perhaps all of us were, but it's worse now. The idealistic world of the financially secure, pillar-of-the-community professional of the last generation presents a lifestyle that is certainly possible but not nearly so probable. Successful competition with third-party eyecare, chains, and price houses will depend a lot upon what we really want to be.

Rural Optometry

Smalltown USA will need independent optometry for a long time. Population-wise we live in the cities, but geographically, America is made up of communities so small they are not attractive or feasible for HMOs or chain outlets.

Optometric Specialties

We have to develop more respect for our own skills, including the fitting of contact lenses. The way a lens fits *is* more important than the material from which it's made. Let people know!

Low vision is unique to optometry. Ours is the only profession that really understands optics and the physiology involved. Furthermore, most people don't actually want to work with low vision patients. The same may be said for children's vision and vision therapy. While many of the new diagnostic techniques are best performed in institutions, there are plenty of opportunities for independent specialists and the judicious use of contact lenses. Sports vision includes contacts but certainly involves much more than that.

Problem-Oriented Practice

There are only two kinds of patients. The majority may be variously considered as easy, naive, price-oriented, or misled. Their usual entry point is the high-volume commercial outlet where, if satisfied, they will indefinitely remain. Just try to convince a penny-pinching two-diopter myope that a lengthy examination and expensive new lenses are in his own best interest. Or worse, try to make the same point with some person who is happily wearing half-eye readers from the drugstore.

The other patient type is a second generation of the first: a difficult person who needs or demands special attention and seeks the problem-oriented practitioner—the fellow with the reading glasses, for example, who decided to wear contact lenses and found out it wasn't so simple.

Problem-solving practices are surviving and prospering. Surveys have shown that fewer than one out of every ten new contact lens patients have not worn them before. In other words, problems, not the basic desire for contact lenses, brings new patients to the door of the small independent practice.

See More Patients

If today's optometrist is to compete with the high-volume medical practice or chain store, the O.D. must indeed work smarter, not harder. The well-run optometric practice depends on good management skills, inventory control, public relations, and the like. If you are working to your highest level of training, these activities must be delegated to an administrator. We will talk about this in Chapter 8.

Additionally, most routine activity *could* be delegated to technicians except that so few are available. There is little incentive for mature, confident persons to enter our field because the pay scale is generally so much lower than it ought to be.

Marketing

This is not for the big guys only. Even the smallest organizations you can imagine have effective and inexpensive marketing programs. It's not hard, for instance, to research your market and your competition, and you can apply what you learn by identifying specific ad media that will reach your potential patients at a cost you can afford.

Worthy Goals

There are winners and losers, says George Sullivan in his old book, *Work Smart, Not Hard* (Sullivan 1988). Successful people have a winning attitude, they look successful, and they do all of the other things you've read and heard about. But, above all, says Sullivan, winners are single-minded in setting and pursuing their goals. Their efficiency and effectiveness make it easier to reach decisions. Without goals, chance and circumstance determine where you go (Locke and Latham 1984; Smith 1986).

Every motivational speaker I've heard (and that includes dozens of them) approached goal-setting in some general ways. I won't argue. Here are some suggestions:

1. *Write it down.* Write each of your goals at the top of a sheet of paper. Think of ways to reach them and write those down too. These are the

intermediate steps and should be prioritized. If your long-range goal is to have a net worth of two million dollars by the time you retire, your intermediate goal might be to start by investing $100 a month in a mutual fund. That's fine, but it's not practice building. Think of the things that will produce that surplus income next year or 5 years from now and put *them* on the list. Long-range goals are achieved step-by-step. Constantly referring to your written objective won't mean much if it is so lofty you become discouraged.

2. *Be specific.* It is important to keep goals specific and measurable. One good way involves dating them, such as "by March 1, I will . . . ." Putting them in writing is essential, but that doesn't mean carving them in stone. Be adaptable when circumstances call for a change.

3. *Have priorities.* The road to success may be a long one, so deciding which steps to take means you must set priorities for your daily activities. I've kept a checklist on my desk for most of my adult life. It is a lot easier than trying to remember them all and keeps the minor pressing issues from getting undeserved attention.

Bear in mind that the ability to totally focus on a clear objective saves the time and energy you might spend planning and starting several different, and likely unsuccessful, modes of practice. This is not to be confused with taking a methodical analysis of potential opportunities.

Personality Goals

There are certain personality traits we simply must include in the goal-setting process.

□ □ □ □ □ Ten Personality Traits of Successful Practitioners

1. An intense desire to succeed. This includes the driving force that keeps a doctor thinking about success when away from the office.
2. Persistence. No matter what happens, goal-oriented people figure they must and will find a way to overcome hurdles.
3. A recognition that we shape our own destiny and don't blame others when we fail.
4. The majority of highly successful people understand that their achievements result mostly from people-skills. They are not always

technically oriented, but they know how to get productivity from those who are.

5. They express their creativity through business actions. Most even have the habit of making notes at night so they will not forget creative ideas that can be implemented later.

6. They accept responsibility for their own decisions, view their business problems as challenges and opportunities rather than frustrations, and expect to have problems because it is part of being in one's own practice.

7. They make bold moves because they are afraid of neither failure nor its consequences. This is why small businesses frequently succeed against large competitors.

8. They enjoy the "winner's image."

9. Most successful professionals really like people. They actually enjoy the interaction, and very few are introverts.

10. They are service-oriented.

All of this boils down to the simple advice to strive for excellence rather than perfection. Perfectionists tend to be frustrated and rarely get anything done. Just do something and do it well.

Be Aware of Cycles

Economists love to talk about cycles—17 years for the locust and 11-year peaks in standard productions. Keeping a graph of annual activities was a genuine help in month-to-month planning in my practice, and over a period of time, revealed some long-range trends. Most notably, that the impact from any major change (good or bad) was felt again after about 18 months. Thus, a 3-year high or low might be anticipated. You will probably figure out cycles of your own, so be prepared to make the most of them.

Marketing Goals

Do you have something in mind? Your ads, brochures, and direct mail should stress your service benefits rather than a list of things you can do. We will talk about that later on. Direct mail is, in fact, a good tool in the right hands when it is carefully planned so recipients will act.

Other promotions include giving workshops or demonstrations or surveying patients and publicizing the results. Repeat patients, their testimonials, and referrals will still account for most of your practice. In their book, *Big Marketing Ideas for Small Service Businesses*, Marilyn and Tom Ross (1990) suggest that responding quickly to calls, letters, and problems should get first consideration, but there are certain marketing tasks that will require outside help, like designing a logo or writing radio commercials. With planning and resourcefulness, they say, a small firm can create a professional and successful marketing program *without a big budget.*

☐ ☐ ☐ ☐ ☐ Ten Marketing Strategies

1. direct mail to patients
2. direct mail to demographic segments
3. community activities
4. printed brochures
     specialties
     general information
     practice policies
5. demonstrations
6. radio
7. TV
8. daily newspapers
9. regional newspapers
10. open houses or parties

Be a Specialist

When prospective contact lens patients consider which type of practitioner to visit, they rarely think, "Do I need an ophthalmologist, optometrist, or optician?" Potential contact lens patients actually think "contact lens specialist" as opposed to a particular brand of vision care, according to Ohio practice management consultant Richard Kattouf. Consequently, he says, well-trained practitioners who have honed their skills with contact lenses are not gaining as many new patients as possible because their specialty remains obscure.

There is certainly no firm definition of a specialist. Certification by various groups includes standards and testing requirements that have little or nothing to do with a positive attitude. But, like the scarecrow from Oz, some people need a diploma to prove they have a brain! A surprising number of successful optometrists, and for that matter M.D.s, finished college after 2 years, but they didn't stop learning. Plan to get good at what you do.

A Lucrative Specialty

Today's contact lens manufacturers are shooting for volume by developing manufacturing techniques that allow them to make enormous numbers of lenses at ever-reducing prices. To keep their pipelines full, they expect practitioners to dispense more lenses so that the volume will make up for lower prices. But, most doctors aren't in a position to do that. Even those who have a fair number of patients won't see enough profit per unit. Opting to push eyeglasses over contact lenses, however, may not be a wise long-term solution because that market is far more competitive. Sooner or later these people will regret abandoning their specialty (Figure 1.1)

Why Don't You Have a Hundred Million Patients?

We've all been to a wedding anniversary, or maybe a Lions Club banquet, where some self-styled social director rings a little bell in a well-intentioned effort to get everyone dancing. It starts with one couple. The bell rings and each seeks another partner, thus doubling the number of participants, so that after the little bell has tinkled six or seven times, everyone is involved.

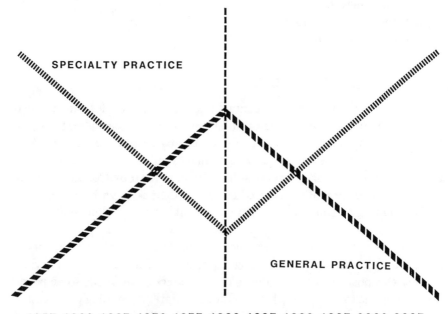

1957 1962 1967 1972 1977 1982 1987 1992 1997 2002 2007

Figure 1.1 Practitioner enthusiasm: specialty practice vs. general practice through a 50-year span. Those who specialized in contact lenses once had enormous enthusiasm for their work, while general practitioners were some-what opposed to the idea. By 1982, specialists began to lose interest as every-one got into the field, but the trend is reversing as fees for difficult cases increase and general practitioners find fitting glasses more lucrative than contacts.

Simple, isn't it? 1, 2, 4, 8, 16, 32, 64, 128, 256, etc. Someone calculated that if a single sheet of paper were torn in half and stacked only 50 times, the pile could theoretically reach the moon, but what's the point of all this?

If you had started practice in 1963 with only one patient, let's say your mother, and if she referred one patient to you during that year, for a total of two, and if each of those people referred only one patient each year, and so forth, by 1980 you'd have had 131,072 active patients. Not bad, but that is only the beginning. By 1991 every man, woman, and child in the United States should have been a patient in your office, and long before the turn of the century, you would be supplying eyecare for every citizen of the world.

Absurd? Of course. Yet the referral of one new patient each year certainly doesn't pose an unrealistic demand. What went wrong?

In every practice there is a "critical point" (Figure 1.2). Somewhere on the giant graph we use to chart our progress, the curve begins to flatten. Everyone, even the rich and famous, reaches the point where they just stop trying for some reason.

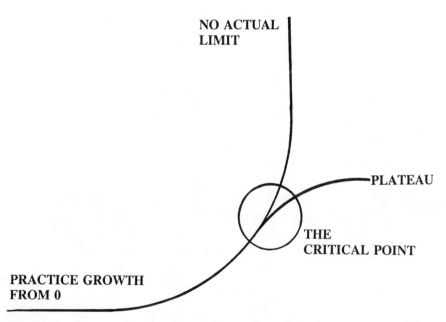

Figure 1.2 Theoretical practice growth. Patients refer other patients, and they refer others, and so on. There are no theoretical limits to the size of any practice, yet every doctor reaches a critical point at which such growth becomes undesirable or impractical. The longer this leveling-off process is delayed, the more successful the practice.

"I'm working as hard as I can," you say. Then efficiency must be your objective.

"But I like what I'm doing now." Too bad, you have unwittingly reached your destination.

"I like what I'm doing, but perhaps some changes would help me get more of the things I want." Ah ha, that's it! Now you are ready for some serious goal-setting.

2

Better Service

The American Management Association says 65% of all retail business comes from existing, satisfied patrons. Happy repeat customers (or patients) are also our best source of publicity.

Outstanding service keeps them coming back, especially so when service is really the only thing we *have* to sell. Most people feel that the doctor's quality and worth are based on patient care, thus good service results in word-of-mouth referrals. Because it costs many times as much to win a new patient as to keep an old one, it is certainly worth finding out what patients want and need, and developing a strategy to meet their expectations. Research by the Marketing Science Institute identified the top five. They apply equally to retailers, lawyers, repair firms, and optometrists.

□ □ □ □ □ Characteristics Patients Demand

1. *Reliability.* Dependable, accurate, and consistent performance is the number one concern. Always keep promises!
2. *Responsiveness.* Prompt service and a helpful attitude follow close behind.
3. *Assurance.* Knowledgeable and courteous employees are important.
4. *Empathy.* Individualized attention and the willingness to lend a sympathetic ear are essential.
5. *Tangibles.* Good physical facilities and equipment must be staffed by well-groomed people. (See Chapters 7 and 9.)

Service begins with a good first impression, but it does not stop there. Here are some specifics.

□ □ □ □ □ Sixty-six Ways to Please Your Patients

1. *Tell them what to expect.* New patients ask a lot of questions on the telephone, but they don't always remember the answers. Even worse, they may

forget to ask about some things. Send a printed confirmation with the appointment time and date. Include those facts that people want to know about your office before they reach the door.

Should children and teenagers be accompanied by an adult? How do you handle third-party bills? What arrangements, if any, have you made for extended payments? Which credit cards do you accept? How long will the examination take? What else will be involved? (See Chapter 12.)

An informative brochure covering specific interests can be enclosed, e.g., information on cosmetic lenses, bifocals, orthokeratology, etc.

2. *Map.* Don't assume everyone knows where you are. Many people will appreciate a simple map showing access to major thoroughfares when they visit your office for the first time (Figure 2.1). This is especially important if you are in a convenient neighborhood, but your actual address on some side street may confuse the first-time visitor. If you relate your location to a major landmark, try to pick something with class. The library or a church beats a pizzeria every time.

3. *Take plastic.* Major credit cards are a whole lot safer than open accounts, and they are much less likely to be a source of embarrassment when a patient falls behind in the payments. Even if you don't want to go for American Express, Discover, Diners Club, or some of the others, almost everyone has MasterCard and VISA nowadays. Suppose they don't? Watch it!

4. *Twenty-four-hour service.* A telephone answering service makes it possible for patients to reach you without disrupting your personal life. The more sophisticated firms may page you with a beeper. Others will simply call your home telephone or wait for you to check in. Many options are available.

An answering machine, for example, can take routine messages and refer patients to a hospital emergency room. Such a system will satisfy most legal requirements, but it comes up short in terms of patient relations. "Call forwarding," especially if you have a cellular phone, is a lot more personal.

Whatever the method, optometrists today have to be sure patients can get help in emergencies. It shows you care.

5. *Quote fees candidly.* Put yourself in your patient's shoes. Maybe the patient is a genuine price shopper or is on a budget or unemployed. Or, maybe the caller just wants to make conversation. But, suppose that person on the phone *really* wants to know how much you charge?

Don't *you* absolutely hate people who give evasive answers when you ask a direct question? Be willing to quote fees, but don't do it in an offhand way. The person who takes inquiry calls in your office must be able to respond in

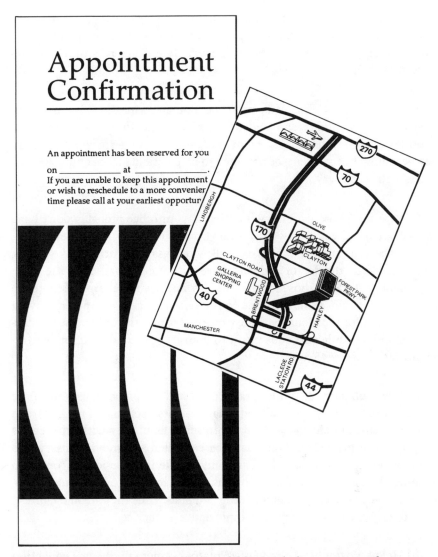

Figure 2.1 Appointment confirmation folder. Including a map with an appointment confirmation will prevent frustration for persons not familiar with your neighborhood.

an unhurried, straightforward, uninterrupted manner. Ask for phone numbers and call back if you must. Mailing a fee schedule is not all bad. When you ask for the name and mailing address, there is ample reason for a follow-up call, just to see "if there are any questions."

6. *Welcome new patients.* A personal note to every new patient shows you care. Not a printed form or business letter, but a small (preferably hand-written) informal note on personal stationery should go out within 24 hours of the first visit.

7. *Time-payment plans.* If a person does not have a major credit card, there is usually a very good reason (and we all know what that reason is). There are some exceptions though, and many successful practices are willing to carry open accounts. In any event, be prepared to help patients to meet unexpected expenses in some way.

8. *Parking.* Those patients who drive to your office probably don't have disposable cars. If you own your building, you've already faced the subject, but even there, a couple of taboos exist. Few things upset patients like a walk in the rain while the doctor and staff have automobiles parked in the more convenient spots. Save those for the patients, and pay the charges if there are any (you might even want someone to run out and "feed" the meter). Paying a lot attendant for additional parking time or getting a ticket because the doctor is behind schedule only adds insult to injury. Or, you may eliminate parking altogether (see #45).

9. *Offer full service.* With a practice limited to contact lenses for more than a quarter century, I usually felt that patients appreciated my expertise in this specialized field and wanted me to send them away with an eyeglass prescription in hand. Not so in many cases! When a frame dispensary was added, we learned very quickly that many people like the idea of "one-stop shopping." Patients want to buy solutions, pharmaceutical agents, sunglasses, nonallergenic cosmetics, cases, and other supplies while they are in the office. Make it easy for them. They will appreciate the service.

10. *ID photographs.* We've kept a Polaroid camera in the data collection room for years and years. New patients and those returning for annual examinations were photographed as a part of the routine. No big thing; the technician simply picks up a camera, takes the picture, and files it in the patient's record.

This identification provides invaluable information from time to time. Looking at the photo during a telephone call adds the personal touch one might expect in face-to-face conversation.

Furthermore, it can be a big help recalling facts once a person is gone from the office. While the camera is in hand anyway, the picture of an accompanying youngster sometimes makes a nice little gift for the parent (see #22).

11. *Take emergencies.* Sure, they're a pain in the neck. "Doctor, I probably lost my lens, but maybe it's still in there." Be there for your patient!

That's what makes you different from the rest. Take the time to remove a foreign body, look at a red eye, or replace a lost lens on a Sunday afternoon. You will have a loyal, enthusiastic patient forever, and you'll enjoy life a little more.

12. *House calls.* No, I don't mean routinely. In fact, you don't even have to make them yourself. Hospitalized or otherwise disabled patients, particularly aphakics with extended wear lenses, frequently require minor acts of attention which can be satisfactorily handled by technicians on the staff. The courtesy has rarely been abused, but many lasting friendships have resulted from some small service performed by a staff member on the way to or from work. The same goes for adjusting or repairing glasses.

13. *WATS line or 800 number.* To be perfectly honest, my office has always been in a large metropolitan area where toll charges have not been a problem. Out-of-town patients were simply advised to call collect. Still, in most communities, I think incoming WATS line service is a fine way to let patients know you want to be helpful. It is now quite inexpensive, and image enhancement alone is probably worth the cost.

14. *TDD.* A special line for the hearing impaired will not bring hundreds of deaf people into your office, believe me! But, it won't hurt either. The TDD is a sort of modem that permits people who also have one to type out a message. The device only costs a couple of hundred dollars, and the telephone company even offers special directory service without charge. The number has long been listed on our promotional material and in the Yellow Pages (Figure 2.2). The service is appreciated by those who use it and recognized by others. It shows we care about *all* of our patients.

15. *The PR card.* In this case, PR means *patient relations.* Not a part of the patient's case record (so it needn't be surrendered in event of any legal call for information), this little card is stapled in the back of every folder. On it the staff makes notations that will be useful to the doctor in conversation later on. Where did you spend your vacation last year? How many grandchildren do you have now? Does your husband have a new job? Do you have a new husband? I think I know your boss. You go to school with my daughter. Etc., etc.

Whatever lends itself to interesting personal conversation is there for reference on the next visit.

KOETTING ASSOCIATES THE

CONTACT LENSES the
EXCLUSIVELY koetting
associates

R.R. Koetting, F.C.L.S.A.
C.F. Castellano, O.D., F.A.A.O.
P.A. Meinell, O.D.
    In The University Club Tower

KOETTING ASSOCIATES THE
  1034 S Brentwood Blvd --------------863-0000
  After Hours Emerg----------------------
  Hearing Impaired TDD Call ---------863-6559

Figure 2.2 TDD phone number. The TDD number for hearing impaired will reach a surprising number of persons who use the keyboard to make phone calls.

16. *Loan outs.* Well, maybe. Patients do appreciate it, and, under certain circumstances, loaning out a pair of reading glasses may be justified. The same can be said for a contact lens of similar, but not exact, specifications when one is lost. Unfortunately, the privilege is frequently abused, and I have known doctors whose inventory is little more than a "lending library" for patients who have never been encouraged to own spare lenses (see #17).

17. *Return privileges.* Far better to suggest spare lenses. Concerned patients can be advised that an unopened vial or unused disposable packs may be exchanged if the prescription must be changed at some later date.

18. *High-tech equipment.* "Next to life itself, God's most precious gift is sight," we've been saying for a good many years, and patients believe it. They want only the best, the newest and most accurate instrumentation, used on the only set of eyes they will ever get. Contrast sensitivity, glare testing, automatic perimetry, fundus photos, you name it! Add at least one new instrument every year so that the examination is a little different each time they come in.

19. *Music on hold.* Almost everyone uses it now. There is nothing so upsetting as dead silence while waiting for a voice to come back. Lots of O.D.s have special recorded messages announcing service in the office, and that is all right too. Using the local radio station isn't. Commercials are not only tacky, but I have frequently heard a competitor's advertisement while waiting for a doctor to come to the phone.

20. *Get feedback.* People like easy quizzes. And, they want to be heard. For more years than I can recall, we have given patients a questionnaire following their contact lens fitting. Ten simple questions that can be answered with a check mark—good, bad, or indifferent—and a postage-paid envelope. The signature is optional, but the last question is most important: "Would you refer a friend to our office?" If the answer comes back "No," we are in trouble, but if it is affirmative, and it usually is, the patient has a commitment.

21. *Fundus pictures.* Granted, Polaroid photographs lack the definition we expect in slides. But, explained to laymen, they are comprehensible, tangible, and *very* impressive, in addition to their usefulness as a part of each case record. At last patients know their doctor is making a complete examination.

And don't forget to remind them that you will refer to this picture during every examination for the next 10 or 20 years. People feel locked into a practice with such a unique record of their eye health. Add a couple of dollars to your fee if you wish, but don't make fundus photography an optional extra charge. The PR value is too great to justify quibbling.

22. *Extra pictures for kids.* Most young persons, especially those in health or science classes, would like to have a fundus photo as a souvenir. Take an extra one and give it to them! The same can be said for patients who have any obvious retinal lesions. You have no idea how many people will hear about your high-tech office as your pictures make the rounds. (You can be sure of identification if a rubber stamp or sticker with your name goes on the back before the photo leaves your office.)

23. *Call the other doctor.* When someone changes doctors, even under the best of circumstances, they really don't know how to go about transferring information. Make it easy for them.

People who are new to the community will be happy to have you handle the chore. If they are embarrassed as they make the switch, you can help simplify the process.

24. *Give a party.* Why not? Jerry Lieblein, O.D., in San Diego throws parties in his office with some regularity. Any excuse will do.

The production of our own contact lens instruction video program gave us the opportunity for an opening night affair attended by staff members and families, in addition to those involved in producing the show. On other occasions, we have entertained people who wore investigative lenses or tried new solutions. The cost of this relatively inexpensive display of appreciation was borne by the product's manufacturer.

It is evidently impossible to give parties for everyone, and selecting key patients requires tact. With a little serious thought, however, you'll be able to see that your invitations reach the right group.

25. *Class projects.* Children in the upper grades, and sometimes those in high school, are frequently involved in science projects that include vision or optics. The AOA's International Library, Archives and Museum of Optometry, can be of help if you need material. Also, keep on hand some literature describing optometry as a career.

26. *Open house.* You have friends and neighbors who have never seen your office. Pick a date and call a caterer. That's all there is to it!

An open house doesn't have to involve free lens trials or glaucoma screening (although you may wish to use that approach). In many businesses, people inform, entertain, or assist the public while maximizing their own exposure. They lead seminars, symposiums, and workshops; give talks; sponsor clinics; provide in-store or office demonstrations; and hold open houses or receptions. A Ford dealer may run an auto clinic to educate persons about their vehicles, while AT&T gives small businesses free telemarketing seminars because it knows that greater use means increased revenues. An open house can sometimes be financed by a frame company that might be interested in replacing all of your samples with theirs for the event.

27. *Recognize referrals.* Thank everyone! Well, you knew that, but try not to send a standard card. Personal notes are much better, and better still, have several different forms so that you don't say the same thing every time. How do you keep track of what you said? Make a copy or note it on the PR card (see #15).

28. *Gifts.* Every practice has some "heavy hitters." People who refer many patients during a short period of time. These friends deserve some special recognition. To set a standard, we sent a gift after the third referral during any 2-year period. These have varied from time to time—flowers, ties, small radios, music boxes, Cross pens, gift baskets, even steaks—always accompanied by a personal note.

29. *Tickets.* A few years ago, we hired a hall and sponsored a harpsichord performance by Dr. Charles Metz, who was with our practice at the time. Tickets went to key patients and were much appreciated. Additionally, the music critic of the *Post Dispatch* reviewed the performance, providing some fine public relations without additional cost (Figure 2.3).

But, you certainly don't have to put on your own show. Most sponsors of amateur productions would love to have you buy a block of tickets. In fact, some will even give them to you in an effort to fill the house.

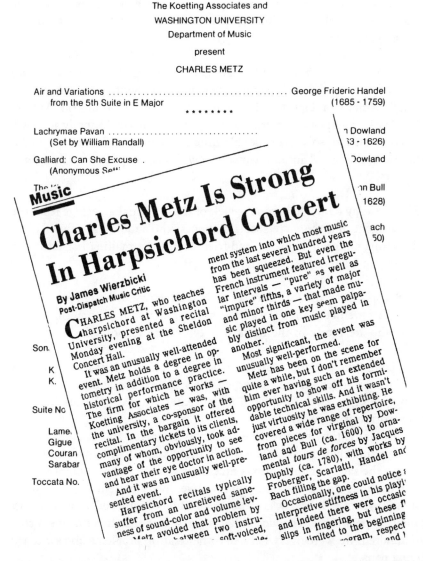

Figure 2.3 Have a special event. Hiring a concert hall provided the opportunity to showcase a talented staff member and reward VIP patients with complimentary tickets. As an added bonus, a music critic applauded the practice as well.

30. *Convenient hours.* The shopping malls and the chain stores have taught a lot of private practitioners what they should have known all along: People do not want to take off from work or pull the kids out of school if they can help it. Saturday morning remains the most popular time of the week, and if you are not in your office, your patient may very likely be in some other office.

31. *Death in the family.* It's a bit morbid, but everyone recalls people who said a kind word at the right time. Watch the obituaries and send memorials. They are appreciated.

32. *Special recognition.* And speaking of memorials, you can help your own favorite cause while brightening the day for a patient by contributing to the AOF (American Optometric Foundation), your Optometric Alumni Association, or your favorite charity. These organizations will happily acknowledge a contribution, so you get double mileage from your deductible dollar. Furthermore, the actual amount won't be noted, so it may cost less than sending flowers.

33. *Birthday cards.* Everyone is sick of these annual greetings from the insurance agent, but there are special patients who should have them: older people, young children, shut-ins, and friends. Put the mailing list into your computer (see Chapter 13). You have the dates.

34. *People in the news.* Don't try to do it all yourself. Assign parts of the paper to staff members and drop a little note when you read something nice. Persons who are rarely in the news will appreciate it most of all.

35. *Long-time patients.* Anyone who has been a patient for 20 years is a special person so far as I am concerned. We started recognizing these people by giving them a new blue-colored folder. After 20 years, the original was usually worn out anyway.

Additionally, they now receive a suitably engraved and packaged Cross pen recognizing their loyalty. The whole thing started when we decided to emphasize the safety of long-term contact lens wear by handing out a conversation piece that would keep the subject alive. Every patient who had worn contacts 20 years or longer was given a pair of lenses imbedded in an attractive lucite paperweight. The idea still has merit, but after handing out a couple of hundred, we were overwhelmed by fabrication problems and switched to giving pens.

36. *Samples.* Everyone loves something free. Don't confuse patients by giving away things you haven't recommended, but there are probably "freebies" available in the brands you are now using—lubricating drops, lens cleaners, starter kits. People love presents.

37. *Out-of-town referrals.* Keep that *Blue Book of Optometrists (Butterworth-Heinemann)* and Academy directory handy. Even if you don't know the doctor personally, chances are you'll be able to find a name or two

you can recommend with some confidence. Patients move. They have friends or relatives who are seeking competent care in other cities. Being helpful will cause them to be grateful and speak well of you, and so will the O.D. who gets the referral.

Each time you have an interaction with an O.D. in another city, mark that person's name in your *Blue Book* directory with a yellow highlighter. This way you will accumulate a quick and easy way to locate the preferred referral target in each city and state in the future.

38. *Be generous.* No one likes to ask for money. If a patient has summoned up the courage to ask for a contribution, do your best to make the experience a pleasant one. I don't think much of discounts. For members of the clergy or underpaid persons working with charitable organizations, I would rather charge the full fee (thus establishing a genuine value for my service) followed by a gift to the church or organization.

39. *Your patients as decorators.* The world is full of amateur artists, and, frankly, most people don't know whether their work is good or bad. You have nothing to lose by encouraging talented patients to hang things in your office. Buy them, trade them for service, or invite artists to show their pieces in your rooms for short periods of time. You can't go wrong supporting culture in the community (see Chapter 9).

40. *Review of charges.* Computerized bookkeeping enables us to supply an annual review of payments without going to a great deal of effort. In our office, the sale of service agreements improved dramatically when the renewal notice was accompanied by a review of activity during the previous year.

41. *Tax help.* This same computer documentation can be helpful in another way. During tax season, people develop a feel of urgency for such information, so it should be supplied without delay. Direct mail presents a serious challenge near the end of each year. Getting anything to stand out from that pile of postal junk people face then takes some ingenuity. We used a simple postcard reminding patients we would be happy to supply the previous year's financial information upon request. It got attention.

42. *Instruction call back.* We hear a lot about compliance nowadays. Almost as though some confrontation must exist. People *want* to wear contact lenses in the right way. Furthermore, they don't always remember what they are told, and being too embarrassed to ask again is only human. Why not call back the next day? (See #46.)

"Mrs. Jones, did you have any trouble taking your lenses off last night?" "Mr. Smith, I just called to be sure you were able to get your lenses on this morning."

43. *New products.* Market testing and investigative programs are everywhere. Letting your rep know you are interested will usually result in an invitation to participate sooner or later. Sure, there is some work involved, but in addition to prestige and some remuneration, it offers an opportunity to reward a few key patients.

Generally speaking, we have found that people enjoy participating in such programs. They have a sense of contributing to the betterment of mankind and are happy to get free lenses or auxiliary products.

44. *Handle complaints promptly.* No, they aren't always right, but it's easier and more cost-effective to please a current patient than to develop a new one. Those with unresolved problems will beat a path straight to your competition.

Let complainers have their say. Don't be defensive or interrupt. Once you are sure you understand, simply ask, "What can I do to make things right with you?"

Studies show that 95% of all complainers will do business with you again if their problems are solved *very* fast. Try to offer possible solutions on the spot. Even when complaints are unreasonable, you are faced with two unattractive choices: give in or suffer ill will and the resulting abuse of your reputation. Better to consider complaints as a valuable resource; they offer an opportunity to make amends and thereby renew and intensify patient loyalty.

45. *Drive-up service.* This obviously won't work in a high-rise or a good many other places. Dr. Wayne Wood of Jacksonville, Florida, took a critical look at his reception desk and found most of the people coming to his office were paying bills, picking up supplies, dropping off frames, or making the trip for some other reason that didn't involve seeing the doctor. As a matter of fact, he reasoned, they didn't even have to come into the office. He took the next logical step and put in a drive-up window.

46. *Follow up on problem solving.* In our office we developed a simple system that is still in use, and I am surprised that more doctors don't take advantage of it. In every examining room there is a stack of printed 3 1 5 cards. Each has a space for a patient's name and a list of possible reasons the doctor may wish a follow-up call (e.g., discomfort, poor vision, red eye, etc.). Months of the year and days 1 to 31 are printed below. Writing the patient's name and circling the appropriate problem and date takes no longer than five seconds.

Technicians deposit these cards with the receptionist as patients leave. They are filed in chronological order, and on the indicated date an assistant pulls the patient's record and reviews it. If no additional information has been added since the visit, the patient is called to set an appointment if necessary (see #42).

47. *Express delivery.* We ship lenses, even solutions, through Federal Express. Out-of-town callers are asked for a MasterCard or VISA number and advised that there will be an additional charge for overnight delivery. The service is optional, but most prefer it in emergencies.

48. *Local courier.* Even people who have spare lenses may not be in a position to dash home from work when they lose one. Most communities have courier service, and even those that do not, have taxis to offer delivery within an hour. An extra $10 doesn't mean so much when someone needs a lens. Get in the habit of offering and promoting this suggestion. You'll be surprised how many times people will act on it.

49. *A large inventory.* Even the price houses begrudgingly send patients to our office because they know we will have the lens in stock. No one likes to make extra trips. Try to make room for ample inventory no matter the size of your office.

Additionally, inventory lenses afford the opportunity to experience the actual sight and feel of contacts during the examination and offer the advantages of same-day fitting when required.

50. *Give information freely.* Good and loyal persons may stray from the fold from time to time. They also return when things haven't gone right with the new doctor. Leaving a good impression cannot hurt.

Your negative reaction to a request for information is never withheld from the patient. "I'm sorry it took so long to get your lenses, but your doctor wouldn't give me your prescription (or he wouldn't call back, or he is just difficult to deal with, etc.)." Don't be a bad loser.

51. *Introduce your staff.* "Which one is ours; waiters all look alike!" So do hospital attendants and optometric assistants. Most of us really *want* to identify persons who are providing service. Name tags, desk signs, and, of course, a personal introduction will smooth the way. Up-to-date pictures of staff members with short biographical identification works if you have a place to hang them. At one time, we prepared a photo album "scrapbook" with information on the staff and placed it on a table in the reception room.

52. *Single chairs.* No one really wants to sit next to a stranger. Avoid benches and couches. Theater-type seating is especially offensive because the single armrest between chairs usually leaves one or both parties uncomfortable.

53. *Refreshments.* Coffee, of course! No great need to have both kinds; most people are satisfied with good brewed decaffeinated, but suit yourself. The same goes for diet soft drinks. Don't use cans or bottles, they contain far too much. Take a tip from the airlines and serve refreshments on ice in plastic glasses. For early morning patients, orange juice makes a fine eye opener.

54. *Cookies.* We like Pepperidge Farm—variety, quality, and light enough for any time of the day.

55. *Telephones.* We have two telephones for patient use in opposite corners of the reception room and a third in the conference room for those who want more privacy. No restrictions. If someone abuses the privilege and runs up a small long-distance charge, who cares? Checking records over a period of time, however, indicates very few unexplained charges.

56. *Take-home magazines.* Some people steal magazines. Most don't. That is why they get dogeared and must be thrown away after a couple of weeks. Better to use little stickers that state, "Please feel free to take this magazine with you if you wish to finish reading an article." (This obviously doesn't apply to the hard-bound "coffee table" books which most patients don't purchase but enjoy reading in your office.)

57. *Conference room.* A multi-purpose conference room/library services all executive members of your staff. Sales representatives, job interviewees, employees, and solicitors all sit at the table, and discussions end there. Thus, when someone calls for an appointment on a business matter, they are shown to the conference room and the doctor or staff member goes to the room. The embarrassment of dispatching a tiresome salesman is eliminated because discussions conclude when the doctor leaves.

During patient hours, the room is available to persons who might wish to conduct some business of their own while waiting. They enjoy the courtesy and privacy involved.

58. *Local authors.* In addition to periodicals, an interest in the community is expressed by keeping local history books in the reception room. "Cocktail table" picture books are always popular, and they show you care about your hometown or state.

59. *Buy a lunch.* Ralph Barstow used to suggest writing a prescription for an ice cream cone for kids to take to the local drugstore. Those days have been gone for about half a century, but, based on my own experience, the idea has merit. During the period when my office was in a building that also housed a good restaurant, we kept an open account there. Patients who were spending some time with us during a contact lens fitting or those who were delayed for some reason were simply invited to go downstairs and have lunch on us. Now, many years later, I am probably reminded more of this single goodwill gesture than any other single promotion activity.

60. *Gifts for children.* You don't have to be in pediatric practice to see lots of kids. Some are patients, some come with their parents, and some are just friends. Rings and fuzzy toys are fine. Paste-ons and tatoos are "iffy." Pens are OK for the older set. Just remember to give them something.

61. *Little chairs.* A children's corner is a long-standing but practical idea. Two small chairs will prove you are human. Subscriptions to children's magazines are not costly, and puzzle books appeal to adults as well. But, be sure to have multiple copies and discard them when they become soiled.

62. *Credit vouchers.* Everyone goofs now and then, and a number of doctors compensate by giving patients a credit voucher for $5 or $10 to be used at some future time. They say it really helps.

63. *Say it with flowers.* So you were behind schedule and the patient could not wait. Or, maybe, the lenses weren't ready as promised. You can apologize, "I'm sorry this is my fault," and your patient will snap back, "I know it!" Try sending flowers.

Every florist has small arrangements suitable for men or women which can go to their offices. A nicer arrangement sent home may be better suited to the occasion.

64. *Your bulletin board.* Keep it up-to-date. Include short articles on vision or eyecare products and news clippings about your patients.

65. *Stay on schedule.* Develop realistic appointment slots. In the automobile service industry, "writers" are the persons who hear your problem, look at your car, and decide how much of a mechanic's time to allocate to your appointment. It is the writer's responsibility to be sure that mechanics stay on schedule. And, so it is with the assistant who books your appointments.

Underbook and you flirt with bankruptcy. Overbook and you face a stream of irritated people who may or may not return. In our practice, appointment scheduling is done on the computer. More important, the telephones are handled by experienced assistants who have a good feel for the length of time that will be required. This is no place for amateurs.

65. *A "family" attitude.* I don't like strange places and neither do you. Our patients are no different. In familiar surroundings they will respond almost any way we want. Expertise is important, but a friendly receptionist may well be your greatest asset.

Everyone loves attention. The most pleasant sound on earth is one's own name being properly pronounced, the more often the better. (See Chapter 7 for more in-depth comments on staffing.)

3

□ □ □
□ □ □
□ □ □

Patient Relations

Confidence Makes the Difference

A trustworthy personality might have meant more to mega-billionnaire Sam Walton than expertise in bombastic salesmanship. Biographer Vance H. Trimble, in his book *The Inside Story of America's Richest Man*, paints a picture of the young Walton as a shy person (Trimble 1990). He achieved leadership in school and in his early entrepreneurial career without hard-sell tactics. He was logical, his ideas made sense, and people wanted to believe him because he gave them a feeling of confidence.

Of Tech and Trust

Consider the acronym TECH. In an ironic sort of way it reminds us that the foundations of successful practice are not necessarily clinical.

Trust
Empathy
Courtesy
Humor

Let's take them in reverse order.

Humor

Being able to laugh at yourself requires a great talent. It tells others you will take responsibility for your mistakes. Revealing some of your human frailties, opening yourself up, sharing your personal experiences—all of these contribute to a good professional relationship.

Empathy

Perhaps some successful doctors don't have it, but they certainly *appear* to. Understanding and compassion are expressed in a multitude of ways—seeing a patient with some minor emergency on a Sunday morning, staying 20 minutes late for a secretary who was tied up in a traffic jam, or "working in" a college student home on break. People must *know* you care.

Courtesy

Common courtesy helps build strong relationships. It also creates long-lasting impressions. By being courteous you'll project the message that you are thinking of someone other than yourself, you are treating others as you wish to be treated, and you are an approachable person.

Trust

The first and most important part of the acronym is trust. It is hard to believe that we don't trust our patients as much as they trust us. When someone walks in the door, or even "price shops" by telephone, they are exhibiting confidence that the job will be done right. Respond to that faith and the patient is yours forever.

Patients Do Trust Us

Advertising, convenience, price, even snob appeal are important. So is the experience and referral of another satisfied patient. All of these factors contribute to the conclusion that a patient has made the right choice. Research by Whirlpool Corporation showed that Americans are six times more likely to rely on the judgment of others than on advertising when they make a buying decision. People in the office are like money in the bank, but we must understand what brings them there. Does a newspaper advertisement simply lure someone in, or does that advertising project an image of importance, continuity, and permanence? The fact is that many persons perceive an advertisement to be a sign of dependability or prestige.

Once patients have subconsciously or otherwise established a desire to spend their money for eye care, the difference in one practitioner's fees over another's becomes relatively unimportant. One survey reported that the overwhelming majority of buyers pays more for name brands because it has confidence in those products.

Continued advertising, like a long-established company name, implies dependability, and patients want to seek service where they feel their trust will be justified. Countless studies have shown that "confidence in the doctor" is the foremost reason given for seeking professional service from chains. ("Confidence" in a doctor whose name they generally can't recall and who is likely to be working somewhere else when they need help again.) Likewise, patients really don't want to shop for a cheaper place to take a prescription. Once a person has entered your practice there is total commitment to you, and that bond will remain there until someone destroys the faith that created it.

In our own office we once put this proposition to the test by interviewing 250 patients (Koetting 1979). We asked them to name the most and least important considerations in the choice of a contact lens practitioner. We asked about specialized limited practice and laboratory services. How about fees and location? Was the referral of another doctor a determining factor? What part of this decision was based on convenience, etc.?

The overwhelming majority (almost 80%) placed "confidence in the doctor" as the number one consideration. "Fees" were in fifth place and "convenient location" was a resounding last.

To be perfectly candid, the results were skewed and the subjects were biased. People who found the location inconvenient were actually denied an opportunity to participate because they had already chosen not to become our patients; likewise, those who might have been deterred by higher fees, etc.

Suppose the same question had been put to a wide-range sample of the American public. Would "confidence" topple from its well-established position? The proposition seems unlikely. A rather convincing four out of five felt it was the most important single reason for making a particular selection. The projection of confidence is the most valuable practice-building tool available, and by a very safe margin. Furthermore, patients have it even before we've earned it.

What People Ask	*What They Really Mean*
How much do you charge for contact lenses?	I want some information on contacts, and this is the way I open the conversation.
How about these lenses I see advertised for $19?	I sincerely want to justify going to your office, but you got off the track during my first question so I guess I'll have to keep talking about money.
What about disposable lenses?	Even though I hate to admit it, I don't know beans about contacts. Please take me off the hook and answer the questions I should be asking.
What if I can't get used to them?	Don't stall around, reassure me quick!

I don't think I could ever wear bifocals.	Please God, tell me I'm not getting old.
Do you have some sort of a time-payment plan?	I'm sure you do, but this is my way of keeping the conversation alive. Besides, I already know you like to talk about money.
Do you think contact lenses might improve my tennis game?	My mirror says I'm getting old and glasses aren't going to help. Please say yes.
Do I have to take them out at night?	Tell me you will teach me how to handle them.
Are they dangerous?	I really want contact lenses, but this time I mean it— Are they *dangerous?*
My husband says I am too old for contact lenses.	If you try to talk me out of it, I'll go to someone who won't.
How long does it take?	Can I make an appointment now?

But Do You Trust Your Patients?

If we become paranoid and cynically assume that everyone comes to us seeking a way to cheat and deceive, we are doing a great disservice to the public and to ourselves. The vast majority is not looking for copies of a prescription in order to shop for cheaper materials. An overwhelming percentage would never try to entrap us in a malpractice suit. Certainly no sane person enters our doors deliberately looking for a fight. Basically, people are really pretty nice.

Mutual trust will go a long, long way. No matter the words any patient may use, no matter how suspicious we may be, if that patient is now in the office, the need for a hard sell is over. It is time to be friendly!

Most people understand a fee for service. They recognize that the cost of glasses (or contact lenses) is not the same as a fee for professional care, and they know the difference. Rarely does anyone ask, "Why is your *examination* more expensive?" That is not where price-shopping takes place.

Gloria Nicola writing in *20/20* said that 50% of the independent optometrists and 32% of those working for chains reported a direct correlation between instrumentation and higher levels of practice revenue. No one would argue that people have confidence in a doctor whose instruments are up-to-date. Automated perimeters and slit lamps lead the list of patient pleasers, but autorefractors, lensometers, and a host of other instruments including glare testers, keratometers, retinal cameras, and tonometers are given credit for practice improvement. Aside from the "glitz," the perception of caring includes the time you actually spend with a patient.

When I have need of professional service—a physician, lawyer, or anyone else—I tend to consider minutes spent waiting in a room alone as a sort of negative factor. Our patients probably feel the same way. On the other hand, as long as something is going on, they think of that as part of the examination. (Although, I've known a good many old-time M.D.s who simultaneously built lucrative practices *and* received patients' confidence by keeping crowds in the waiting room doing nothing at all.) Surveys show most optometrists in both commercial and private practice allocate the same half hour for an examination. Trust and confidence evolve from the way patients *perceive* the care they get.

More Than Half a Century

Long ago I read Dale Carnegie's timeless classic *How to Win Friends and Influence People* (Carnegie 1936). He said then, and it is still true, that people are not creatures of logic but of emotion. We influence other people and gain additional confidence by talking about what *they* want and showing them how to get it.

□ □ □ □ □ Carnegie's Key Points

- become genuinely interested in other people
- make the other person feel important and do it sincerely
- honestly try to see things from the other person's point of view
- make others happy while doing what you suggest

Carl Sewall runs a $250 million-a-year agency in Dallas and has been called the country's top luxury-car dealer. Like so many top merchandisers, he values each customer by what he thinks they will spend in a lifetime. In this case, he figures each one is worth $332,000 and offers tremendous service to be sure they will go nowhere else.

In his book, *Customers for Life*, Sewall admits to borrowing and modifying business ideas and suggests that readers do the same (Sewall and Brown 1990). Disney taught him to keep the place immaculate, and from Neiman-Marcus he got into the habit of always saying "yes" to customers. The third of his ten commandments sums up his philosophy: "under-promise and over-deliver." Don't just keep your word, exceed it!

Patients come to us confident we can fulfill their needs. If we face each of them with a dedication to nurturing that emotion into loyalty, they will become our "customers for life."

4

Niche-Marketing

Forty years ago my hometown boasted the world's largest brewery. Its only bottled product was called Budweiser, and every drop was made in St. Louis. Anheuser-Busch's market share hasn't really changed much since then, but the company now has many breweries and more than a dozen kinds of beer.

Company executives wisely recognized that different markets exist and that selling must be tailored accordingly. So it is with optometric practice. Most of us can only see a limited number of patients anyway, so why not be selective? For my part, I'll take presbyopes who want contact lenses. But, before we get into that, let's learn to speak the language.

Niche-marketing simply refers to efforts directed toward only one specific group of customers, clients, or patients. It is sometimes called "segmenting" because the ad campaign zeros in on some particular group.

Segmentation is a current buzzword with special significance for independent practitioners. There is hardly any way for even a large advertiser to reach everyone. The challenge is even greater when the promotion budget is limited. Thus, striving for a specific portion of a market makes pretty good sense. Identifying and reaching that group, however, involves some specific techniques that most of us are not very familiar with.

Psychographic classification, for example, is a relatively new term for developing prospective patients by psychological makeup—personality, attitudes, leadership, independence, etc. This "pigeon-holing" can be useful in both ad writing and media planning.

If you don't understand how to classify people in that way, don't worry. Many public relations and advertising firms still rely on *demographic* or *geographic* segmentation, and these less sophisticated approaches are certainly more comprehensible to most of us.

In lay terms, *geographic segmentation* simply means picking a neighborhood, city section, town, country, or otherwise, where patients are most likely to be found. Within each area we recognize the common characteristics of the people who live there. Downtown patients, for example, might be business people who are most effectively motivated by rapid service or lunchtime and early evening hours.

Demographic segmentation—dividing a market into categories such as age, sex, income, education, occupation, family size, race, and the like—is useful in making media decisions and commissioning creative material. Most newspapers, magazines, radio, and TV stations know their readers', listeners', and viewers' habits. They will supply these with great enthusiasm if they can approximate your requirements. In an established practice the demographics have been predetermined. Learn to recognize them and work within that framework (or try to change them if you wish).

Advertising in a publication or on a television show that delivers a good audience of 25- to 35-year-old business people isn't likely to be effective if you wish to reach graying Americans, and, conversely, don't waste your money on easy-listening stations or garden club magazines if you want to develop an upscale practice.

Where Are You Coming From?

Jeffery R. Davidson offers some advice on self-marketing in his book *Blow Your Own Horn* (Davidson 1987). The secret, he says, is to develop skills that will make you a valuable professional and then promote them in a way that will earn the respect and success you deserve. Any workable plan must begin by defining what you have to offer to the niche you have selected. An effective marketer may even create a niche, but that takes a lot of work.

Find Your Niche

Let's say there are two department stores located in the same part of town. At first glance you might say they are head-to-head competitors. But, what if one department store is Saks Fifth Avenue and the other is Cheap Sam's Discount House? Clearly, the nature of the stores themselves makes them noncompetitive—one appeals to upscale business and fashion customers, while the other serves those interested in lower prices and commodity merchandise.

So, understanding who *you* are is crucial to defining your trade area or niche. What kind of patients do you want—low-, middle-, or high-income? What about education, sex, attitudes toward optometry, etc.? Without defining a lifestyle, effectively targeting promotional activities will be nearly impossible.

□ □ □ □ □ **Typical Niche-Marketing Segments**

Possibilities include people who
   live downtown
   are college students
   work for certain companies
   have young children
   live in the vicinity of your office
   are home owners
   belong to unions
   are young adults without children
   are young professionals
   patronize the arts
   enjoy spectator sports
   are price-conscious
   belong to neighborhood social clubs
   work nights
   live in the suburbs
   belong to preferred provider organizations (PPO)
   belong to a certain ethnic group
   are white-collar employees
   are blue-collar employees
   have certain religious affiliations
   play golf or tennis
   are presbyopes
   have some political affiliations
   are on Medicare
   are in military families
   belong to country clubs

Remember, your niche can include any combination of groups that are not mutually exclusive or severely restrictive (like presbyopes who play tennis and work for IBM). But, when selecting a target, one must realize that there are certain things even advertising *cannot* do. Regardless of what you have been told, don't expect miracles.

□ □ □ □ □ **Advertising: Things It Cannot Do**

Advertising cannot sell where need is absent. Neither contact lenses nor eye care will have great appeal for persons who do not think they have a vision problem. This situation calls for "two-step advertising." In other words, potential patients must first become aware of the need for an eye examination. Institutional advertising, such as "Save Your Vision Week," will help; so look for a tie-in.

Advertising cannot sell someone "out of the market." Anyone who is completely satisfied with a doctor, or who has just paid for a workable lens prescription, won't give much attention to your promotion.

Advertising cannot satisfy a patient. Only your service and materials can do that. If someone made a mistake, it won't be corrected by promotional activity.

Advertising cannot save an incompetent doctor. (But most of them think it can.)

Selecting a Print Medium

Where to start? In one way or another, the choice of an ad medium depends upon the target market and your budget. Compare newspaper and magazine rates by cost per thousand (CPM): the cost of having your ad seen by 1000 people in each publication. If the circulation is 50,000, for example, and your ad costs $500, your CPM is $10. However, it may be worth paying a higher rate for a publication aimed directly at your niche.

Newspapers

Newspapers have never been my favorite means of communication because they lack the "class" I'd like associated with my image. For certain groups they can be effective though; so, if you want to advertise in them, just remember to avoid the "clutter" in the Wednesday edition's food ads and Friday's entertainment ads (Figure 4.1). Also keep in mind that a newspaper's 1-day lifespan is its biggest disadvantage.

Magazines

Magazines stay around longer and thus sell longer. Besides, ads look better on slick paper. If you are into the "big time" and want to reach a high-population area, most national publications have special editions that go to one geographical zone. I was particularly pleased with the results of our ads in some local, small-circulation magazines and with the secondary impact of an airline's in-flight publication. Take fair warning, though, this form of promotion is not for beginners.

Direct Marketing

Direct marketing is the mass mailing of promotional literature to residences or businesses. The approaches to direct mail vary. Some "mailers"

Figure 4.1 Never miss an opportunity. Name recognition comes in many forms and sometimes in other languages.

(companies that specialize in the direct-mail business) types or hand address the envelope or use a name and street address for the return so it won't look like "junk mail." Others grab attention by using a brightly colored envelope or a teaser message that doesn't give away the whole sales pitch that's inside.

If you can get people to open the envelope, a good letter can generate a respectable amount of business practice. It's also the easiest part of the package to customize for different target groups. A letter has to supply information while persuading people to part with their money. By incorporating the traits of your niche prospects, with the important benefits of your own professional care, you should be able to develop an attention-grabbing opener and, if possible, an enticing P.S. When prospects find the beginning and end of interest, they will go back and read the entire letter.

Brochures

A brochure can be used for direct mail, to respond to inquiries, and as a handout to persons in your office. You may also use it as a mailing piece to confirm appointments. This will be covered in Chapter 8 when we talk about communications.

Outdoor Advertising

If you just want *exposure,* outdoor advertising is probably a winner. Whether you use large billboards or small subway and bus cards, your message will be in front of prospective patients on a daily basis, provided you know your market well and select a heavily trafficked location.

Suggestions for Print Advertising

Advertising creates visibility and demand for your service, but you don't need a Madison-Avenue budget to create a strong presence. The formula is sometimes referred to as the 3 Cs:

Continuous
Consistent
Comprehensible

Continuous. Frequency is the name of the game. Several small ads are better than one large one. It may take 3 or 4 months before they begin to pay off, and you have to do it often enough so that when prospects think of eye care, or contact lenses, they think of you.

Consistent. Maintain uniformity in your presentation.

Comprehensible. Your ads must be clear and easy to understand. They should explain service with a "you" rather than a "me" or "we" approach, always emphasizing benefits. Use punchy verbs and adjectives without exaggerating.

☐ ☐ ☐ ☐ ☐ Four Basic Types of Print Advertising

1. *Institutional.* These ads aren't meant to elicit a direct response. Professionals use them to build recognition and trust.

2. *Advertorials*. Eye-catching ads that look like news articles, and say "advertising" in tiny letters across the top or bottom, are ideal for service organizations seeking a low-key profile. Such "articles" are often read more than conventional advertisements.

3. *Display*. These ads use space, bold headlines, and possibly illustrations to forcefully tell your story. Make sure your name and phone number are visible and include your address and, possibly, credit card logos, office hours, and testimonials. Some display ads even use a coupon to increase response.

4. *Classified*. Low-priced by the word, a good classified ad shouldn't be too skimpy. Spell out enough benefits to entice readers to respond. Promise something beneficial, then ask for inquiries. Track results by asking callers how they heard about you. It may sound more cost-effective to buy a series of ads, but start with a single insertion until response tells you if the ad and the publications are working.

Choosing a Broadcast Medium

Radio and television can generate practice at a cost. It will usually take 3 months before you get results, but radio spots are an affordable way to reach a small geographic/demographic area. Select stations whose programs appeal to your niche. Adults are reached during morning and evening drive-time, while teenagers listen evenings and weekends.

Don't shy away from TV advertising because you think it's too expensive. Prime time certainly *is*, and you may not be able to afford a professionally produced commercial or to sponsor a particular program. There are alternatives though, like running spot commercials adjacent to programs that are likely to attract the audience you want.

Generally, spots on local stations are more affordable, and, of course, late nights and daytime are less expensive than mid-evenings.

Radio

Older adults looking for health care are quite likely to respond to radio advertising, according to a study by health-care marketing expert Dr. Robert Van Dellan of Cadillac, Michigan. About 47% of older consumers surveyed by Van Dellan's firm said they would call a physician in response to a radio commercial.

Older consumers, he says, want quality and professionalism, not a fast-talking salesman. Dr. Van Dellan offers these tips on radio advertising:

- Identify your service early in the commercial and mention it a few times during the ad.

- Provide the listeners with a specific benefit.
- Be prepared to spend some money. Run your ad frequently and rotate it to a different time slot to avoid overkill.
- Don't use spokespeople unless you are certain they have a sterling reputation in your community.

Radio reaches almost everyone, but it is especially effective with mature adults, even though they are more likely to spend their evenings watching TV. Certain radio formats make up at least half or more of the nationwide audience. The benefits of radio advertising over other medias include its price, targeting ability, and frequency, says Maury Webster, executive director of the 35 + Radio Committee, New York. The wide variety of broadcasters, he points out, makes it a more highly targeted medium than television. Any major American city may have 5 television stations, yet still have 20 radio stations. Thus, advertisers can market their products via a nostalgia music format, country music, classical, religious, talk radio, or all news.

Mediamark Research reports that more than 60% of the nostalgia listeners are over age 50. The second most popular adult format, as you might imagine, is easy listening. Radio offers the advantage of getting a message out hourly or even several times an hour. Magazines and newspapers provide only a daily, weekly, or monthly frequency. Moreover, radio gives the advertiser the entire stage while the commercial is running.

Buying Time

According to the Radio Advertising Bureau, Americans spend nearly 3 hours each day listening. The Bureau's vice president, Daniel Flamberg, says, "Radio is a selective medium. People self-select which station they want to hear." It is easy to determine which station is reaching the people you want for patients because broadcast salespeople love statistics. They are endlessly checking demographics and ratings. They can tell you about the age, income, and ethnic background of their listeners and when they are tuned in. What's more, they can tell you where the bargains are.

If your budget is limited, say so. I wanted to zero in on "big spenders," so I picked stations that catered to a mature upper-income audience. If your preference is young adults or price-conscious people, that is OK, too. Because of the variety of radio formats available, it is easy to select a group.

□ □ □ □ □ Ten Ways to Make Radio Pay

1. *Free Time.* The FTC doesn't require stations to air public-service programming as once was the case, but most stations still broadcast interviews. They are aired about 5:00 A.M. on Sunday mornings, and almost any message

concerning vision will be acceptable. One needs to do little more than volunteer.

Why go to that much effort when so few people will be listening? A PR person once put the whole thing in perspective for me: "I'll bet you would take off a couple of hours to talk for a Rotary or Kiwanis Club meeting with no more than 50 people in the audience. We know there are three or four thousand people listening every hour of the night, and there are no distractions."

Getting on a health call-in show isn't as easy, but if you handle it well, you will be invited back.

2. *You don't need to be an instant expert.* There are free consultants at every radio station; so use them, it won't cost a thing. They will help you write copy, produce commercials, and come up with a schedule. Unless you want something really special, the conception and production of the commercial are generally included as services.

3. *Understand how commercials are sold.* Most stations sell 30- and 60-second spots. Additionally, a station might sell either a separate 10-second announcement or a 10-second tag.

As a general rule, 30-second spots tend to cost 80% of what 60-second ones do. When stations construct their programming, they allow for a certain number of interruptions per hour. So, it doesn't matter whether it's a 30- or 60-second commercial, it's still an interruption.

4. *Keep it short.* Radio spots can be purchased in almost any length. Name recognition is effective and may be good enough. Your address or telephone number with a short slogan takes only 10 seconds. Repeated with some frequency, the ad will cost less than you might think.

5. *Listening habits will help.* People who listen to easy-music stations tend to keep them tuned in longer than people who listen to rock-and-roll. If you are scheduling an ad campaign, you can get by with fewer commercials on a "beautiful-music" station than one of the others.

6. *Do it yourself.* Almost all broadcasts nowadays are taped on cartridges or "carts." Try recording a short message at home and listen to it. Ask a couple of friends to give you a frank opinion. If the outcome is favorable, tell the radio stations you want to use your own voice and ask for a staff announcer (who will probably be supplied without charge) to repeat your name, address, and telephone number at the end.

7. *Try an inexpensive format.* Questions and answers are a fine way to get a message across, especially if you have no training. The announcer simply asks, "Dr. Jones, a listener has asked if contact lenses are available for persons with astigmatism," or "A gentleman from Nashville wants you to tell us about bifocal contact lenses." An inexpensive 1-minute spot allows time for two or three short questions with a professional effect.

8. *Repeat your message.* Studies show that people aren't conscious of a message until they hear it at least three or four times. Even then, being conscious is a far cry from acting on it. You can never repeat the information about your practice too many times.

9. *Public-service announcements.* Local charitable activities are always seeking publicity. Any benefit can be promoted and followed by an announcement: "This public-service message was brought to you by Dr. John Smith, optometrist, etc." Not only will Dr. Smith gain community respect by supporting the event, he also will win the enduring gratitude of the organization's members.

10. *"Sawtooth."* Running ads on alternate days, weeks, or even months has been shown to be almost as effective as a regular broadcast schedule (and is another way to make radio pay without spending a lot of money).

Pick the Right Station

Although some people look at media-buying as a science, it is still an art. Look at advertising from all medias—radio, television, newspaper—and then make common-sense decisions that are right for you. Consider the station's role in your community.

Sometimes a business decision to advertise on a particular station comes down to more than numbers. There are several markets around the country where stations have a particular role in the community. They have been there for a long time, their call letters reflect where they are located, or they cover the local sporting teams. Give these matters some serious thought. If it is important for you to reach the audience of a station which carries the local football games, that station may be the best radio buy for you, even though it doesn't have the largest number of listeners.

Your radio audience is held captive when shaving, showering, or riding in an automobile. When someone has me on hold, I've even heard commercials from a competitive company. Believe me, the "golden age" of radio didn't end with Jack Benny and Kate Smith. It is still with us.

Television

Sure, we all know that TV is the most effect advertising means available today. Not necessarily cost-effective, but it works, and that is the reason that big companies spend billions of dollars to reach the "couch potatoes." With a few exceptions, TV advertising is beyond the means of most independent practitioners. Furthermore, television is *not* a good niche-marketing tool. I really don't recommend it over radio, but if you want to try TV, there are some things you should know.

Television Reaches Women

For all practical purposes, prime time is out. Even though most of your female patients probably work outside the home, they still watch a lot of daytime TV. The average woman spends 4 hours and 45 minutes exposed to television every day. Assuming 17 waking hours, that means 28% of a woman's life is influenced by the tube.

In preparing copy, be aware that women account for more than 65% of health-care purchases. In the book *Reaching Women: The Way to Go in Marketing Healthcare Services*, these common characteristics are listed (Alpern 1987):

- Women want to be addressed with respect and empathy in a way that shows that they are educated, successful, productive, and valued.
- Their time is valuable. Offer appointments at unconventional hours (early morning, dinner time, or Saturdays) to gain loyalty.
- They like to make educated purchases. Become a credible source of eye-care information, presenting it in an inteligent and understandable manner.
- Most women like to be in control and feel that they have choices.
- Their confidence and trust will be won by consistently delivering quality services.
- They are value-oriented and will spend more for desired quality, but promotion of the service must be sincere, honest, and compelling.
- Women respond better to results rather than to means. Information must center on direct benefits.
- They consider their children as priorities and want the best to help them achieve later as adults.

□ □ □ □ □ Eight Things You Should Know About TV Advertising

1. *Public-broadcast channels.* So-called "educational" television has a lot to offer. For all practical purposes, the credit that goes to underwriters and sponsors is no different than commercials carried on other stations. The rates are somewhat lower, and, additionally, there is a public perception that sponsors support culture in the community. Because there are few commercial breaks, yours will stand out.

Be selective if you can. Choose celebrity performances and unusual events just as you would on any other channel. My simple rule-of-thumb involved selecting programs *I* would like to watch as a means of reaching persons in a similar socioeconomic bracket.

2. *Cable.* According to Bill Crowell, general manager of the Cable Advertising Network, 1988 marked the critical year when more households in the nation had cable than did not. Almost 2 billion dollars goes into cable advertising annually.

"Subscribers choose cable every time they pay their monthly bills. Usually, when you make a financial commitment to something, you use it," says Carl Gentile, the Network's director of sales and marketing. Besides offering a captive audience, cable delivers a targeted market segment as well. It is, in fact, an advertiser's dream: affluent audiences with more disposable income (35% of the viewers earn more than $40,000 and tend to be in upper management or own businesses).

3. *Ten seconds is enough.* Television is expensive, no doubt about it. It is also very effective, and if you haven't tried, you'll be surprised at how much recognition you can get in 10 short seconds. No time for a message here, just your name and phone number with a picture in the background. My favorite was a pretty girl with green eyes stepping out of a Rolls-Royce convertible, while the voice-over observed, "When people in St. Louis think of contact lenses, they think of The Koetting Associates!" We will talk about that again later.

4. *Independent channels.* We ran the short spot I just mentioned during late-night movies—the kind you will find on small independent channels. Most independent channels' rates are low, and the station will even help you make your commercials. Unfortunately, the neighbors in your time slot might be pretty "tacky"—food slicers, dating services, and used-car dealers abound. Before you get involved, try to find out the types of ads that could be broadcasted before or after your spot.

5. *Off hours.* Low-budget advertisers buy time at 2:00 A.M. because it is cheap and reaches some of the people some of the time. Try it for a few weeks; response will tell you who is watching.

6. *Tag on.* Your media representative can tell you when news or special features will cover eye-care subjects. You may wish to buy some time immediately following the broadcast, but beware! This is not an original idea, and others will do the same. To make matters worse, I've been interviewed on TV only to discover in dismay that a price ad was broadcasted immediately following my remarks. Such uncomfortable situations are best avoided by getting assurance before you go on the air.

7. *Anyone can make a tape.* In virtually every area there are schools and not-for-profit organizations that teach videography. For experience and/or a small remuneration, these institutions welcome an opportunity to make low-budget commercials. Many optometrists have also used such services to produce contact lens–training videos and the like for in-office use.

8. *Pilots.* The opportunity to appear in a product-oriented program doesn't

happen often, you may be sure. But because I've had the experience on several occasions, the possibility certainly exists. You will be gambling your time and effort against whether anyone ever views the program, of course, but there are a variety of small companies trying to develop product-oriented formats to show on broadcast TV, cable, or even for sale to your peers. Most are on a shoestring budget and cannot find doctors or staff willing to invest their time without assurance of remuneration.

When the producer has completed the show, it will be given to a broadcaster and played for audience reaction. I don't think any of mine have done well, although I really don't care. They didn't cost me a cent, and they've been seen by lots of viewers. If the opportunity comes your way, don't pass it up.

When to Start and Stop

A marketing campaign has a definite life cycle. It grows, matures, then withers. As time elapses, the effect declines and a fresh campaign is indicated. This new effort will not only start the cycle moving upward again, but will build on the success and recognition your previous activity had generated. An ongoing professional marketing program, when carefully developed and executed, will establish a specific theme and, through repetition, can produce recognition and success.

Because successful marketing is an ongoing process, you should arrange at least 4 full weeks of uninterrupted exposure for any campaign. For optometric care, the most effective days of the week are Tuesday, Wednesday, and Thursday (beware of those food special editions). Individual experimentation may be a good idea, to establish your personal formula for maximum effect. Don't expect the phone to jump off the wall with the first insertion. Sit back and try to relax during this growth stage. Repetition is the key, and your potential patients have to be continually exposed to it.

□ □ □ □ □ Seven Steps to Marketing Success

1. *Develop a concept.* Discover or create something about your practice that makes you different, and then promote it the right way. Bifocal contacts, a family plan, some kind of special service, problem-solving, etc.—whatever you decide on, keep your promotions believable.

2. *Continuity helps image building.* You can talk about selection, services, or ongoing value, but the most effective is usually a mix of image and promotional advertising. This combination can produce powerful results, It's crucial to keep your name out in front of people during periods of nonactivity so they recall it when they need you.

3. *Don't look for instant action.* Building consumer awareness and perception of value takes time. Plan early and stick to it. Stay with your message so that when patients finally do need your service, it will be perceived as a true value.

4. *Stick with one medium before you try another.* Most advertisers try to do too much with too few dollars. By attempting to impress everyone, they spread themselves too thin and end up reaching a minimum number with a message that says too much. Don't worry about radio spots and TV commercials if you are involved in a print ad campaign. Deciding on the proper medium depends on the demographics, geographics, and psychographics of your potential patients.

5. *Planning ahead saves money.* Professional media negotiators can usually buy space in advance — 3, 4, even 6 months is not unusual. You'll get far better rates and savings of up to 50% or more. But, always set a few dollars aside for any unplanned promotions or unexpected time or space (in the business this is called "distressed media"). Use co-op advertising dollars (sharing the cost of an ad with a supplier or manufacturer) whenever possible to increase your budget.

6. *Budget for growth.* Many advertisers do not invest enough. For many years I have advised that 7% of the gross income should be allocated to promotion — 5% for advertising and 2% for public relations.

Unfortunately, these figures work only if the practice is well established. You can't do much with 7% of $30,000. But, 7% of your *projected* gross will do a lot. The more you invest, the faster you grow.

7. *Sell value.* If you want to develop a price-oriented clientele with limited means and no loyalty whatsoever, you may think price advertising is important. I won't argue that point right now, except to caution that if you are selling price, you should always attach a strong sense of value. Brand names are important to consumers. Give them names and comparison prices, *real* reasons to buy.

Interviews

In this book, the topic of interviews will be covered several times, because it is the best way to establish your image in the community and to reinforce or reassure patients. When it comes to low-budget marketing, print or broadcast interviews just can't be beat.

I really believe that using a PR firm to arrange interviews is the best way to handle the matter. (We will discuss dealing with a PR firm later in this chapter.) No matter how good your message is, you will get little or no response if it does not reach the right editor. You must know where to go with your story. Even if you already know reporters and editors in your city, there is no guarantee you will get coverage. Learn about media in your area by reading newspapers and magazines carefully. Listen to radio talk shows and learn which reporters cover the "beats" that will be targets for your message. Keep track of bylines of health articles. Most small newspapers and stations do not have a medical reporter, so you will deal with a writer who covers other matters as well. It won't be easy, but in this case you should tactfully try to review the article before it goes to press.

Be Prepared

Do your homework. Never attempt to "play it by ear" when a reporter calls. Make sure you are clear on the subject to be discussed. This allows for some anticipation of what might come up and what you will want to say. You can never be sure what a reporter will ask, so it's helpful to gather as much background information as possible. Consider recruiting your staff to role-play with you, drilling you with tough questions that might arise.

Now, with the interview approaching, shut the door, hold all calls, and give yourself time to clear your thoughts. The most important thing is to plan what you want to say, because you are being given a grand opportunity to do so.

Define your objectives. Write down the most important message you want to communicate. It's best to limit yourself to no more than three main points and support each with three or four subpoints.

These must be presented in an interesting way. Have some anecdotes or analogies to back up your main messages, because reporters like to hone in on colorful quotes. Try to learn the format of the program if your interview is scheduled for radio or television. Listen or watch to get a feel for the program.

OK, warm-up is over. Now it's time for the interview. In the next few minutes you'll either put your practice's best foot forward, or plant it squarely in your mouth.

□ □ □ □ □ **Twenty Ways to Conduct an Interview
and Make Sure You Get Interviewed Again**

1. Be frank, reporters appreciate it.
2. Don't warp facts; the truth will come out eventually.
3. Expect to be quoted, even when you least expect it.
4. Don't play favorites, it creates resentment.
5. Talk from a consumer's point of view; use words that can be understood.
6. State the most important facts first.

7. Use personal terms like "I" instead of "we."
8. Always tell the truth.
9. Never try to mislead, it creates ill will.
10. Have the facts or story ready, reporters hate wasting time.
11. Always be available.
12. Don't say "off the record" or "this is not for publication." If you don't want to see it in print, don't say it.
13. Do not be evasive, it only stimulates more probing.
14. Be sure of facts, names, and figures.
15. Trust reporters, but don't assume they are on your side.
16. Do not beg, it lowers your status.
17. Don't complain about minor errors, many cannot be avoided.
18. Try to help reporters, they are human too.
19. Don't complain if your story isn't used; there is always a "next time."
20. Never get into a fight with the media. You will lose!

Press Releases

Press releases are an inexpensive and effective (if you do it right) way to reach a lot of people. They are fine for coverage of fairly routine events, but even if printed in their entirety, they are usually short and often wind up buried where few readers notice them. More substantial public interest can be raised by a feature story, especially if you are trying to reach a specific niche.

Placing a feature story, that is inviting a journalist to write about your practice, involves convincing that person that it would be of general interest.

□ □ □ □ □ Feature Stories: What to Suggest

1. *Be observant.* Pay attention to the local media and which reporters cover professional care and human services.

2. *Look for an angle.* Consider the visual possibilities of the story. Even one with limited news or human interest value is likely to appeal to a TV station if it action and color. Don't be afraid to suggest photo possibilities to newspapers.

3. *Evaluate the human element.* Readers or viewers like to learn about people, technical advances, and new procedures if they understand the benefits. Including children or the elderly makes your story more attractive.

4. *Be flexible.* If a reporter appears interested in another angle than the one you originally planned, go along with it. More important, if the reporter is not interested, don't burn your bridges by becoming angry or defensive. Find out what the reporter would like to talk about.

5. *Speak up.* When something important happens in your field, particularly contact lenses, don't be shy. Call the media and tell them you are ready to talk about it. *Please, please, please, however, be certain your position will agree with one officially taken by the AOA or your local optometric organization before you talk.*

6. *Letter to the editor.* A letter responding to coverage of professional issues is an easy way to generate exposure. Whether it is used depends on the size of the publication and clarity of the message, but take a positive approach. Praise coverage you agree with and phrase criticism tactfully.

□ □ □ □ □ How to Increase the Odds of Getting a News Release Published

- Include a headline that attracts attention.
- State a problem that everyone can identify with and tell how to solve it.
- Make it no longer than two typed double-spaced pages.
- Include quotes.
- Provide a photograph (preferably black and white), reproducible artwork, a visual design, or even a logo to establish an association.
- Include a caption for all photos.
- Address it to the proper editor. (If in doubt, send it to the managing editor.)
- Include your name and phone number.

Finding the Right People

All agencies and consultants are not created equal. As a matter of fact, there is a significant difference between those that are geared toward effective advertising and those that specialize in public relations. Only a few are pretty good at both, so you must make a choice. But how?

Ask around. Talk to people who have small businesses in your community and make a list of those agencies whose work has been effective. Contact them briefly with your plans; ask to see samples. Learn as much as you can. Whenever you have the opportunity, ask broadcast personalities or newspaper writers which agencies *they* respect. Ultimately you must talk to the firm's clients, and consider asking past clients why they dropped out. (But don't base your decision on an isolated case until you've heard both sides of the story.) Before we get into the things you should do, here are a half dozen you should avoid.

□ □ □ □ □ **Six Ways to Stay Out of Trouble with an Ad Agency**

1. *Don't be suspicious.* Try not to challenge everything by continually asking, "What if this doesn't work?" Be prepared to continue the program and have a contract. In other words, the direct route to failure involves a lack of respect for the integrity of the people who will be working with you. Show some trust.

2. *Select a firm that understands your field.* An agency with a fine record of advertising automobiles or pizzas cannot apply the same approach to eye health and contact lenses.

3. *Have a clear idea of expectations and responsibilities.* Do you want them involved in research marketing or just advertising? Do you have a good idea of who your prospects are, or do you expect the agency to tell you who they are? Do you want them to develop marketing strategies or just implement the plan? How aggressive should they be?

4. *Fix a firm budget.* Deciding what you can spend from month to month blocks any form of long-range planning.

5. *Never assume that all account executives are alike.* Your representative is the key person in your relationship with an agency and must understand your business and goals. You must feel comfortable with the agency's representative to make things happen.

6. *Don't think that a handshake is good enough.* Once you have narrowed your selection, a presentation is in order. Asking for free advice about your practice will usually produce something that is worth about what you pay for it. A low price is no bargain if the results are ineffective.

When You Start Serious Advertising

If you really don't know anything about it, become a good observer. Watch television, listen to the radio, and look carefully for work you like. Call companies directly and ask, "Who handles your advertising?" Most will be happy to tell you. Then make up a list.

Set up a meeting and get to know people in the agency. In addition to the quality of their creative work, find out how much of it is done in-house. It may be wise to contract with an agency capable of accommodating your needs for newspaper and magazine ads, direct-mail campaigns, television and radio, or any other vehicle you select. A firm with its own typesetting equipment, art department, and composing facilities can save time, and you will have fewer worries with deadlines. That also saves money, but don't rule out smaller operations. Higher fees at the large firms might easily justify your looking somewhere else. Little agencies generally handle fewer clients and can offer more personalized service with a flexibility that is simply unavailable with the big outfits. Much work, for example, may go to good part-time artists who work for less.

How About Fees?

For the moment, let's not consider PR and look at advertising alone. The standard 15% commission is not so standard anymore. An increasing number are negotiating rates based on the amount of work required for a particular piece of business. When you are looking for bids on some project that involves creative work, don't seek more than three bidders, and expect to pay for some of their time, or you won't get much. Few will want to speculate on landing your account until you've become better established.

Choosing a Public Relations Consultant

The rules are just about the same as when choosing an ad agency, but in this case, you will not be so concerned with artistic, creative, and mechanical ability. Your PR representative *really* has to understand.

□ □ □ □ □ What to Look for in a PR Consultant

When seeking the "right" PR consultant, follow these steps:

1. Determine what you want to achieve.
2. Conduct a thorough search by asking people in your community.
3. Contact a principal at the firm you select and request a meeting. (Don't settle for a representative selected by their telephone operator.)
4. Be certain your representative will have no conflict of interest with other accounts, while still trying to get someone who has health-care PR experience.
5. Plan to spend at least 2 hours with the persons who will be working with you.
6. Don't feel uncomfortable about admitting you are talking to other agencies.
7. If you can't decide between two firms, ask for specific proposals.
8. Once you've made a decision, nail down the fee structure and length of the contract.

PR Fees

Public relations firms typically have three fee options: retainers, minimum monthly fees, and project fees. Which one you choose will depend on the services you require.

The *retainer fee* is a flat monthly charge, paid in advance. The fee remains the same regardless of how much or how little you use the agency's services.

A *minimum monthly fee* is a flat monthly fee based on an estimated number of hours of work. Like the retainer, it is billed in advance, but in this case you will also pay for hours worked over and above the minimum.

Project fees involve situations where ongoing service is not required. I have used this approach many times to determine what an agency can do. Hiring an agency to develop a single campaign of some sort (a mailing, a brochure, some community project, etc.) afforded me the opportunity to sample the firm's work without entering into a long-range contract. Regardless of which fee arrangement you choose, it is wise to make sure it is documented in a letter of agreement.

In summary, when you are getting started with professional marketing help, be selective. The relationship needs good chemistry to work, and a small agency may be best for you. Be honest about your budget and don't expect a complicated proposal on "speculation." A one-time start-up marketing package can cost $2,000 to $5,000. Consulting may run from $50 to $100 per hour. Don't expect instant results; publicity and promotion have a cumulative effect that can't be quantified.

Do-it-yourself Advertising

Maybe its a little too much like being your own lawyer, so it won't be strongly recommended here. If you really want to handle matters yourself, though, there are some things to consider.

Dealing directly with a media sales rep cuts out the middleman. In fact, says Kurt Wildermuth in an *Eyecare Business* article, media salespeople and account reps can be helpful and even integral to the success of any promotion program . . . if the advertiser manages the program and not vice versa. He offers some advice if you're taking charge personally.

□ □ □ □ □ Advertising: Doing It Yourself

1. Determine what you want the advertising to accomplish and which medias are most likely to accomplish it.
2. Request rate data, audience figures, and promotion deadlines from all potential media.
3. Determine your advertising budget allocations annually.
4. Develop a 12-month plan, using a month-by-month calendar to key in insertions and deadlines.
5. Allocate 10% to 15% of your ad budget for unexpected promotion opportunities.

6. Make media purchase decisions based on advertising that works rather than working with friendly reps.
7. Listen to reps for information that might be useful.
8. Be skeptical about "inside" information and "special" deals.
9. Be flexible in changing media or reps when results are lacking.
10. Put media sales reps to work for you, and make the final decisions yourself.

The Telephone

A "memorable" number will give any practice an edge. A fine example is 345-2020, but most of the available 2020 numbers have long since been grabbed by enterprising practitioners. The idea is certainly no more novel than the Humane Society's 456-PETS or a waterbed store using 789-REST. Such numbers contribute to the pulling power of an advertisement but don't do much to establish confidence in the doctor.

Repeated digits or those ending in 00, such as 5555 or 7800, lend an appearance of stability and are more easily remembered. Our own office number, 863-0000, is easily recalled and has been responsible for opening conversations with hundreds of people who comment on the unusual combination. I've often wondered why so many optometrists seem afraid to discontinue an inconvenient, unattractive phone number simply because they don't want to spend a few dollars to update their stationery. Our experience would indicate that a change is worth many times the effort and expense involved in obtaining it.

We've talked about telephone coverage several times, so I won't go into it again, except to point out that when patients call any optometrist at 9:15 on a Thursday morning and get no response, they are faced with several conclusions: (1) the dialer may have called the wrong number, (2) the doctor may not start hours until 9:30, or, perhaps, (3) the receptionist is very busy with another patient. It may also mean that (4) the office is closed on Thursday, (5) the doctor is on vacation, (6) the phone may need repair, or (7) the optometrist just doesn't give a darn. Depending upon the caller's needs and/or enthusiasm, the person will either try again later or seek the services of someone else. A recorded answering device can solve many problems, but there is no substitute for a live answering service.

Telemarketing

Pretty crude, but it works for some people. Cold-calls to strangers have a poor track record. If you are trying to develop a particular niche, say presbyopes who live in a certain part of town, calling persons over a certain age with specific prefix numbers is a relatively simple matter. Computers make it easier, but put yourself in your target's shoes before the calling begins. On the other hand, calls to your own patients have been proved effective and well worth the effort.

Yellow Pages

So much has been said on this subject there is scarcely anything to add. I am pleased to share four rules which have served me well. This may, in fact, be the most important thing you will read in this book.

□ □ □ □ □ How to Get the Most Out of the Yellow Pages

1. Invest in the real thing. Don't waste money on directories that aren't distributed by your own phone company.
2. A single line, standard, small-type listing is only half as effective as a boldface listing.
3. One-column-wide box listings, regardless of size, in the proper alphabetical position are twice as effective as boldface. Even better if they contain a logo and/or special information that will make your practice stand out (Figure 4.2).
4. Anything larger will probably not be as cost-effective. Big ads frequently don't appear on the page with others offering the same service or in the proper listing order. Furthermore, studies have shown size contributes very little to their persuasiveness.

□ □ □ □ □ Developing Your Marketing Plan

1. Select a practice name and logo.
2. Print stationery and business cards to reflect your image, and use the same style in all of your printed material.
3. Office signage must be tasteful but overt.
4. Imprint patient information materials for handouts to patients.
5. Send letters to key people such as referral sources, friends and relatives, and community leaders (from your computer or a business letter service). Cover any subject you wish, but make sure they know you are there.
6. Join organizations such as Rotary, Lions, or other service clubs; chamber of commerce, a church; or special-interest civic groups.

GERNSTEIN MARVIN L
Co-Lens Inc
Practice Limited To Contact Lenses
And Eye Examinations
Ophthalmological Center
   211 N Meramec Av ------------------**863-1700**
   If No Answer Call ------------------------388-5523
Ghormley N Rex
  South County Office
   10103 Concord School Rd -----------843-5700
Guhl-Midtown Optical 634 N Grand ----533-4781
Hartig David B 2533 Woodson Rd---------423-3874
Hartig Jas W 1745 N Highway 67 -----921-6360
Hartig Richard 144 W Adams------------821-9440
HERBOLD W L OPTOMETRIST INC
  2627 Telegraph Rd ---------------------**892-3321**
Hoelting Carl R
  11704 W Florissant ---------------------921-7000
HUFF DOUGLAS L

PERSONAL EYE CARE
FOR THE ENTIRE FAMILY
   • CONTACT LENSES •
    • SPORTS VISION •
COMPREHENSIVE EYE EXAMS
   DESIGNER FRAMES & SUNGLASSES
  EVENING & SATURDAY HOURS AVAILABLE

HUFF DOUGLAS L
  Just North Of Hwy 40
   777 S New Ballas------------------997-3833
HUFF DOUGLAS L 4401 Hampton Av--**353-6171**
Hurd Kathy K 65 Charleston Square ---928-6929
Huth W L 9842 Regency Pl---------------638-2660
Iverson-Hoelting Eye Clinic
  11704 W Florissant ---------------------921-7000
J J Optical 3819 Vaile --------------------838-3311
KIEFER WM F & ASSOCIATES INC

WILLIAM F KIEFER SR O.D.
WILLIAM F KIEFER JR O.D.
RAYMOND F FADA O.D.
ROBERT H HENDERSON O.D.
CHRISTOPHER G SEEP O.D.
MICHAEL K BILLINGS O.D.

4305 Butler Hill Rd ---------------------**487-4744**
36 Hampton Village Pl -----------------**752-1440**

Figure 4.2 Column box listing. A column box in the Yellow Pages is often the most effective way to advertise. The listing is large and readable, a professional degree can be included, and most important, it appears in the proper alphabetical position. Larger more expensive ads are frequently found on unrelated pages.

   7. Advertise in community papers.
   8. Develop a brochure describing your practice.
   9. Begin regular mailings to the groups listed in #5 and #6, plus new acquaintances and patients.
 10. Begin a broadcast media program.

               OR

 10. Hire a PR consultant.

Keeping Score

How can you tell if all this effort is paying off? How can you tell what will work and what won't and when a program should be discontinued?

Part of the answer is very simple. *Everything* works, but some activities are more effective than others. After a few years of practice, I became accustomed to new patients saying, "I met you at a Lions meeting 4 years ago," or "I once read an article about your office." Don't expect immediate results, but if you are not getting any feedback after 6 or 8 weeks, something is probably wrong. The acid test really involves your year-end bottom line—5% to 7% of your gross income spent on promotion should be producing a 14% to 20% annual growth.

5

The Presbyopic Market

I've probably too often quoted Willie Sutton, who said he robbed banks because "that's where the money is." It's a fact that in America 80% of the wealth is controlled by persons who are over 50 years of age. Furthermore, they are all presbyopes and need some visual correction. So why not contact lenses?

Projections indicate they will make up less than 2% of the contact lens market, and that is reason enough to "go for it": *Almost all of the people who have almost all of the money haven't tried contact lenses.*

How Do You Find Them?

Where do you start? In your office! Gear your image and your thinking toward patients over 40 who are not looking to the department stores, chains, or discount houses for contacts. Identifying these people may be easier than you think. Just as men and women frequently perceive the same product or service quite differently, those who don't intend to spend much money feel more comfortable with specific kinds of promotion.

Gaudy ads with boldface prices represent "their" kind of eye care. Conversely, the "that's where the money is" segment likes the clean uncluttered advertising one expects from Mercedes or Saks. Throw out everyone else? Of course not. I'm only suggesting you recognizing the potential and cultivate it.

No one, especially a presbyope, wants to wear contact lenses. They just want to read without glasses, or to put it another way, they want results and are willing to pay for it. How often have you heard a patient implore, "Doctor, I don't mind spending a little more if you can fit me with a lens that will work"?

With this level of motivation there is small wonder some investigators can report 35% success while prescribing the world's worst soft lens bifocals. Yet, paradoxically, many market analysts still predict no more than 1 contact lens patient in 20 will be over 40 years of age at any time in the foreseeable future.

There are a thousand ways to sell presbyopes on contact lenses, of course, but one method we use is a patient pamphlet (Figure 5.1). Many other types of pamphlets are available, but this is the one we use. (The copy in the brochure follows on pages 68–69.)

Figure 5.1 A patient information pamphlet for presbyopes.

What Is Presbyopia?

"Prez-be-o-pe-a" is a condition which limits our ability to focus easily from distance to near after we reach age 40 or so. Some people read without difficulty and use glasses to see far away, but most wear them only for near tasks. Benjamin Franklin usually gets credit for solving the problem with bifocal spectacles, but as you might guess, contact lenses involve many additional challenges.

How do contact lenses correct presbyopia?

There are four ways:

1. When a relatively weak bifocal is involved, the improved optical efficiency of conventional contact lenses eliminates the need for separate reading and distance prescriptions so one lens power will work for both.

2. Infrequent use or special task situations may call for occasional rather than sustained need for a bifocal. In this case, "half-eye" reading glasses are prescribed to wear over the contacts on an "as needed" basis.

3. Present day optical science and research have improved bifocal contact lenses so that many more persons can now wear them successfully. (More about that later.)

4. Monovision, the most common method of correcting presbyopia with contacts, involves fitting one lens for near and the other for distance vision.

How Do Contact Lens Bifocals Work?

There are two broad classifications. *Simultaneous* vision bifocals bring images at two or more distances to focus in your eye at the same time. The *alternating* kind work somewhat like bifocal glasses, moving to permit sharper near seeing when your eyes point down into a reading position. Simultaneous vision lenses may be *annular* with powers arranged concentrically, or *aspheric* without a specific power zone but focusing light rays from several distances at the same time. The *diffraction* bifocal incorporates a precise series of concentric diffracting rings splitting rays from distant and near objects to form images on the retina.

Alternating vision contacts are usually constructed like bifocal spectacle lenses with a distance portion on top and the near portion on the bottom. The exact size is critical and a variety of controls are used to prevent rotation. Because these must move or "translate" to work, the adherent quality of soft lenses limits their usefulness with this design, but rigid contacts work quite well.

What Is Monovision?

Monovision is a system where one eye is focused more clearly for distance and the other for near. The brain selectively learns to focus on the clear image while disregarding the blurred one, a natural phenomenon which goes on constantly as we subconsciously ignore things we don't want to see. In the case of bifocal eyeglasses, for example, we learn to look through the top part of a lens to view distance objects and through the bottom for near.

Despite what you might suspect, judgement of distance is not seriously reduced. In fact, this contact lens optical system provides such a good range of focus that trifocals are usually unnecessary. Furthermore, the absence of a dividing line is a great convenience for most people.

What If I Only Wear Reading Glasses?

People who need reading glasses usually wear a single contact "invisible monocle" on one eye. That way, it is always there when you need it.

How Long Does It Take To Get Used To Monovision?

No two persons are alike and occupational requirements differ, so no certain time can be promised. Some people see well immediately, but most will not adapt fully for six to eight weeks.

Which Is Best For Me?

During your examination, the doctor may try several systems, and additional options may be explored depending upon the way you adapt. Every step will be geared towards providing a practical and realistic alternative to glasses. Studies show that 9 out of 10 presbyopes who begin wearing contact lenses are still wearing them satisfactorily a year later.

Contacts are a great alternative to glasses of any kind. Additionally, they eliminate the need for matching frame styles and colors with wardrobes and accessories. Whether you are at home, the office or dining out, contact lenses will help you feel confident about your appearance and your vision.

Do As I Do

If you are a presbyope, in-office marketing obviously includes setting a good example. Nothing is more effective than wearing contact lenses yourself. In-the-same-age-bracket conversation comes easily, but what is a younger optometrist to do?

Advice to respect your elders may at first glance seem hopelessly out of date. There is a fine line between friendly and familiar, though, and crossing over can have disastrous results.

For many years our office staff followed a simple rule: If the patient is younger than you are, use the first name. If the patient is older, or if there is any doubt, address the patient with the proper title of respect (i.e., Mr., Mrs., Miss, Doctor, Reverend, Judge, Sister, etc.). Even if a patient insists you call him "Joe," your staff is not excused. Everyone secretly loves this little touch of formality.

We will talk more about this later; for now let's just say most patients over 50 have a strong but subconscious idea of the way a doctor should look — not clearly what professional appearance should be, perhaps, but rather what it should not be. Trying to imply a familiarity with current clinical techniques by wearing sports clothes in the office will bomb out. Like it or not, judgment of your technical competence is based on your appearance.

Some other advice really applies to everyone, but especially so when the patient is older than the doctor: be pleasant without trying to be a comedian. A couple of years ago I heard Meredith Morgan offer some very sound advice to young O.D.s: "Remember," he said, "chances are you don't know a single joke your older patients haven't heard before."

Let's Talk Monovision

Don't get hung up on theory. Because the concept of monovision is so universally understood, prescribing a contact lens to correct monovision will enjoy excellent acceptance if you give it a chance. In our office, a careful study of 200 patients showed that over 90% adapted well and were continuing with contact lens–monovision correction after a year of wear. I am personally convinced that almost all problems result from practitioners' own insecurity and feeling that it probably won't work.

Nero has been depicted viewing events at the Circus Maximus through an emerald monocle. Whether he was compensating for myopia, presbyopia, or a serious need for sunglasses is uncertain, but he was undoubtedly among the first to learn that one doesn't have to wear a corrective lens before both eyes. I used this system routinely from 1964 (the year I became a presbyope) until I retired and have watched at least 15,000 satisfied patients meet the challenge. We refractionists, schooled in the fundamentals of binocularity, find it hard to believe, at first, that reading with one eye does not ordinarily cause headaches or severe discomfort. (Experience also indicates that many people probably don't care whether they read or not; so the motivation to be rid of glasses often makes slightly reduced acuity quite acceptable.)

What It Isn't

A couple of misconceptions ought to be corrected right away. Monovision is not *occlusion!* Acuity, in any area except the central 2 or 3 degrees of the central field can be reduced to the extent that 2 diopters of ametropia is all but indiscernable. In other words, seeing through the near correction at distance or near objects through the distance correction in no way resembles total occlusion. At its very worst, the blur experienced by uninitiated monovision patients is no greater than that experienced when a presbyopic person tilts their head back to view some distant object through a bifocal seg, and even then it affects only one eye.

Most wearers exhibit surprisingly good stereopsis, but the fact remains that *stereopsis is not depth perception.* In judging distances, stereopsis provides only a minor clue and is virtually ineffective at optical infinity. In other words, driving a car or flying an airplane doesn't require binocular vision.

Show and Tell

The most valuable aspect of correcting monovision with a contact lens may well be the ease of screening that occurs during the examination. An immediate reaction indicates whether the idea is acceptable. Seeing how things are going to look requires no imagination. Patients can be asked if they would feel confident wearing such a prescription—Would they feel safe driving? Or, might this sort of lens interfere with their occupation? On the other hand, trial lenses for bifocal–fitting are rarely available.

Annular segs and aspheric progressive addition lenses have enjoyed only modest popularity, even after 30 years on the market. Whether rigid lenses or soft, their record of success is far from noteworthy. No less an authority than Irvin Borish once observed that true simultaneous vision lenses are rarely acceptable. (They work, he thinks, because patients use the near part of one and the distance part of the other.) Most practitioners will agree that, in the past, simultaneous soft lens bifocals have been a near disaster, even though newer designs do hold some promise.

Multifocal contacts are evidently the correction of choice in certain cases. Those facing critical seeing tasks, such as driving a truck or proofreading, may be better fitted with segmented bifocals. Persons who have useable vision in only one eye have no real choice. Even so, the hyperope who shifts from spectacles finds less accommodative effort required to read, and a great many younger presbyopes get along quite well with a single-vision correction. TRY IT!

Don't settle for any one approach. Thomas Edison often said, "Try everything." Noting that he had attempted to use over 600 different materials for a light-bulb filament, he assured his backers that he would try Limburger cheese before he gave up. Try everything? Too many people leave our offices before we try *anything*.

Strangers in Your Office

Simultaneous vision or translating bifocals, monovision or even reading glasses, presbyopic-marketing begins right there in your examination room. Now, let's talk about those folks who have never been to your office: upscale older adults.

Well groomed and conscious of their appearance, these people need to be pampered—they want to be chic and they expect your service to be first class. Price advertising won't attract this group.

These people go to the best restaurants and order "off the menu" items without asking the price. They don't want economy, they want excellence, and your image must be just that if you want to attract them. They are not demanding people, but they will not accept second-rate service. We call their segment "contact lenses for grown-ups."

A few years ago I engaged a marketing research firm to make some recommendations. After looking the field over, these experts noted what we already knew: namely, that most contact lens wearers are young females. They drew an entirely different conclusion, however, by pointing out that mature males must therefore constitute the greatest untapped market segment. They even suggested an attractive slogan to reach this group.

The result was "Contact Lenses for Executives" (Figure 5.2). We advertised in business publications, airline magazines, service club bulletins, and on drive-time radio. We experienced a gratifying increase in the number of presbyopic fittings and a substantial improvement in the socioeconomic level of our patient base.

Do it with class! The Rolls is still rolling. Airlines sell first-class tickets, and people buy them. Develop a strong image in your community. Reach the right people. Sponsor an art exhibit, underwrite a concert, participate in a fund drive, volunteer for things! Willie said it best, "that's where the money is!"

Start Now

Presbyopia can be corrected in a lot of ways. The worst estimates of success indicate that one out of three presbyopes will wear contacts if they try them. A competent, experienced clinician can easily raise that figure to 70% or 80%. Because you can't see everyone anyway, the presbyopic segment

Figure 5.2 Contact lenses for executives. Male presbyopes represent the toughest target for contact lens advertising. A public relations consultant recommended the key word *executives*. This very effective ad ran in airline in-flight magazines, business journals, and service club newsletters.

ought to be well worth your marketing efforts. After all, half the nation is now "over-the-hill." Perhaps we suspected that, but statisticians have verified 1989 as the critical year. There are now more people over 40 than there are persons who haven't faced that landmark birthday.

All presbyopes are not created equal. Lumping older people together as a monolithic market is a common error that frequently backfires on advertisers, and can just as easily trap those of us in the eyecare field.

Who Are the Older Americans?

We older people don't deny our age, but our attitude toward it is surprising. If you ask the majority of us "graying Americans" how old we think we are (if we didn't know the right answer), about three-fourths would say something that is 75% to 80% of our actual chronological age. Cognitive age—the age people *feel*—is where our attention belongs.

Behavioral expert James Gollub points out that our values and general style of coping is transferred from early adult years into later life. Our outlook is influenced by what we were, he says, and that makes us what we are. He is deeply involved in studies that attempt to define consumer behavior by analyzing the times in which groups of consumers matured.

Segmentation is the big word in marketing today, and in a similar fashion, David B. Wolfe, founder of the National Association of Senior Living Industries, breaks the older-adult market into several segments (Wolfe 1987).

Younger people, Wolfe feels, get satisfaction by owning products such as cars, video equipment, and homes. The *possession experience* is a strong focus in their lives, especially the first time they buy something like an automobile or VCR. As they grow older, many people shift their focus toward services or *catered experiences.* Travel, restaurants, art, and major sports events assume a large role in their quest for satisfaction. An older person is also likely to hire someone to take care of mundane chores, such as mowing the lawn or painting the house. Those who spend most of their discretionary dollars on possessions are most often under 40. Those who spend more on catered experiences tend to be 40 to 60. After that age, discretionary purchases are influenced by what Wolfe calls the *being experience.*

He observed that, despite their claims, children of the 1960s only took time to "trample the roses." They won't really be ready to smell them for another 20 years. But their attitudes are changing. They are emerging from a period characterized by disproportionate emphasis on material possessions. These "Baby Boomers" now want to be pampered. They pursue almost anything that might make them younger looking, more beautiful or handsome, and slimmer.

Younger adults, say 35 or so, are oriented toward acquiring tangible signs of affluence. They buy things because they need them. They buy things because they want them. But most of all, they buy things because they want other people to know they can afford them. However, the number of persons in the younger-adult market rapidly declines as the population balance shifts to more Americans over 40 than under 40. It has been suggested that this shift will also have an affect on sales of tangible items and is quite likely to be felt by many suppliers.

Next Comes Luxury

In any event, the Boomers have moved out of the younger-adult phase and into the next one. The urge to collect the signs and symbols of acquisition have been left behind. They don't want to keep up with the Joneses; they want to *be* the Joneses.

These are the people who want service. They hire babysitters, even maids, and lawn service. They take spa trips. They go to restaurants more often, and wherever they go, they like for people to wait on them.

So how does this apply to your office? Simple, patients want attention! Remember that the children of the 1960s identified with nonviolence. Many still compromise to confrontation. If they don't like the way you practice, some will avoid an argument by just going to someone else. Staff courtesy, attention to detail, and recognition are more important than ever.

We've already talked about your telephone, for example. Having a round-the-clock answering service is a reflection of your own personal interest in every patient, and your receptionist's voice represents concern for a generation of people who want to be pampered. Combining a paging system with your car phone will have genuine appeal here.

Perhaps I sound like we are dealing with invaders from some foreign land, and that certainly isn't the case. Still, lives are molded by ideals that continue into adulthood. If you belong to this group yourself, topics of conversation present no problem. To those of us who do not, recognition of a few characteristics may be helpful.

☐ ☐ ☐ ☐ ☐ Some Persistent Characteristics of Baby Boomers

1. *Self interest.* Some grown-up "flower children" haven't stopped searching for deeper meanings, and they spend heavily on self-improvement.

2. *Involvement.* Remember there are still a good many former protestors who subconsciously remain skeptical of authority. They need to feel involved and believe that what they do will really make a difference.

3. *Rights of others.* The marchers for civil and women's rights remain firmly committed to equality and many causes espoused by small groups.

4. *Ecology.* The "save the planet" generation is still seriously interested in health, natural products, and the environment.

☐ ☐ ☐ ☐ ☐ Today's Presbyopes

In summary, there are five special characteristics to keep in mind when you talk to today's new presbyopes.

1. They tend to be well informed and won't stay in your practice if they sense a battle over their concerns. They want their needs fulfilled, their objections acknowledged and honored, and they do not expect to lose an argument.

2. They care less about the benefits of your professional care than how the end result will support their current lifestyles. In other words, they do not want contact lenses, they just want to read without glasses.

3. They want to make their own decisions, assisted by a friendly staff. They want to pick frames and alternative services without feeling pressured and hassled.

4. They expect individual attention from, and personal relationships with, you, the doctor and with your staff.

5. They like, and will pay more for, superior personalized service. When it is missing, they will simply go somewhere else.

Remember people have been getting presbyopic since the dawn of time. And ever since the invention of the plus lens, someone has been providing their first corrections. That part hasn't changed, but, otherwise, your approach will have to be a lot more personal for the next few years.

Who Are Today's Presbyopes?

The 96 million Americans born between 1946 and 1964 represent one-third of the U.S. population (Cetron and Davies 1989). Immediately preceding them is an older group of graying citizens almost as large. You have plenty of experience with this generation. They may or may not share the Baby Boomers' values—some are traditionalists, holding to the concepts of the 1930s, 40s, and 50s, while others behave totally like their somewhat younger counterparts. Telling them apart presents a serious challenge. They do have one thing in common: a strong take-charge attitude that reflects impatience. That is another subject, however, so for now, let's just talk about today's presbyopes— the ones you will be seeing for the first time during the next 10 years.

This mobile generation enjoys a unique freedom of movement and creative lifestyle. As a general rule, they prefer control of their own time more than the security and rewards of even long-term employment. Evidence of what was called the "me" generation certainly includes a reduced number of persons who are joining lodges, churches, service clubs, etc. Becoming a Shriner, a Lion, or captain of the bowling team was big stuff when I started practice. Such things just aren't as important anymore. Life is not the same.

There is a segment of this generation that seeks interpersonal relationships, philosophical introspection, and the conscious seeking out and contemplation of the joys of living. Product- and service-generated feelings provide less satisfaction for this group, as intangible things grow in importance — things like getting in touch with oneself, enjoying a sunset, taking a walk in the woods, or having a friendly conversation. The somewhat older presbyopes we see in practice tend to fall into the latter camp, and they cannot be treated exactly like most members of this generation, even though they have many things in common.

Emphasize Lifestyle

Because lifestyles and experiences are more important than things, these over-55 people must hear about the benefits of everything. Personal appearance and fun have become important, and contact lenses, properly presented, may be very appealing. Insurance plans and health ads that emphasize negative results are a turn-off. Let's face it, we know we are getting older, so we tend to skip over messages that emphasize bladder control problems, hemorrhoids, etc. Those in my generation prefer advertisements that emphasize the appearance of youth and show mature persons relating to young people. We want to see elderly people being a part of things instead of simply being singled out as a separate group.

A Big Market

More than half of the advertising by America's 100 largest companies is now targeted to an older market. But, aiming at a target and hitting the bulls-eye are not the same things. Uninformed efforts have led to some classic market failures. The maker of Gerber baby foods, for example, once tried to market their product for denture wearers. When a company analyst observed that a lot of older people were buying conventional strained vegetables, he reasoned, quite accurately, they were eating it themselves. Unfortunately, the analyst failed to understand a basic point: If a grandmother buys baby food, the cashier will think she is buying it for her grandchild. When she buys adult baby food, she advertises the fact she wears dentures. The product bombed.

Many professionals with experience in the older market marvel at how little influence cost makes on purchase decisions. While many seniors are not dollar-sensitive, they are value-sensitive. In other words, if they like a product and think it's worth their money, the price tag is only a matter of affordability.

To older persons, the value of a discretionary product or service is determined by its potential for enjoyment. A stereotypical image of the miserly, price-conscious senior citizen is seriously misleading.

They Are Individuals

They want monograms, not brand logos on their clothes. Mature people have negative reactions to emotionally stimulating ads and resent suggestions that they buy something because it is "in style." They consider luxuries, like a Mercedes, an enhancement of their lifestyle. But, they will not buy expensive brand-name household products because these are seen as wasteful extravagances—simply paying too much for something that is utilitarian. Older people see differences in companies (or doctors) rather than in specific products. They don't seek out great variation in treatments or lenses, but they do look for security in the background of the practitioner or company, tending to trust products that look like something that was familiar in childhood.

Jerry Bird, president of Centennial Bank in St. Louis, established that institution to deliberately encourage older depositors. The institution is based on the philosophy that senior citizens have two major wants: quality, or perceived quality (in other words, their money's worth), and personal attention. They want to make their own judgments. In a recent Roper Organization poll, 68% of adults age 60 or older said they did not like commercials that named the competition or claimed superiority by direct product comparison. Seniors want to decide for themselves.

Understanding the way mature personalities react to a restaurant, for example, provides a fine clue to running a successful optometric practice. Experts tell us that senior citizens will pay little attention to the meal itself. They *expect* that to be good. If the reservations are made in a surly manner, however, or if the parking is not convenient, or they must wait too long, or the noise level is offensive, etc., they just won't come back. No matter how good the meal may have been, they can afford and expect good food. They are impressed by the *other* details.

David Ward, senior vice president of Saatchi and Saatchi, a New York public relations firm, says that people in the 50-plus age category are highly critical of traditional advertising because it has been targeted to older people and features older characters. He says people age 50 to 64 have been ignored by advertisers and those 65 and up are victims of stereotypical portraits. They want to feel like they still have the power to control their own lives and that age hasn't robbed them of it, even though the great depression instilled certain values that include respect for hard work and saving money.

Don't Forget Reading

Older people read more, not because they have more time, but because they feel it is more important than younger persons do. Hence, good eye care takes on added significance because they want to be productively involved. Likewise, print advertising becomes more important. They tend to read community newspapers and newsletters. In direct mail to seniors, I am told, pictures are essential.

Reaching Older Patients

Many banks have a senior citizens "advisory" board, and the idea is not without merit in optometric practice. Why? Besides showing you care, the feedback could be quite valuable—perhaps your chairs are too deep, the restrooms inaccessible, or, maybe, your staff just doesn't understand. Many employers have begun to include older persons on their staff as a means toward better communication.

The McDonald's organization suggested a minimum of six people over 55 should be on the payroll in each of their locations. It isn't a matter of saving money, it simply improves relations with older customers. The Days Inn chain reported a 30% increase in business after they instituted a policy of employing older adults. Optometric offices can do the same.

Make the place comfortable. Older patients who are not otherwise physically handicapped are embarrassed by problems involved in maintaining balance. Carpets shouldn't be too deep, and chairs should be a little higher and firmer than you might expect, with arms for some added support. Unobtrusive handrails are secretly welcomed. And don't worry about physical contact. Younger people have been taught not to let anyone touch them, but most older folks are used to it and like the idea of shaking hands or having an arm put around them. This certainly applies to maintaining balance when stepping out of a refracting chair or being seated before a slit lamp.

In St. Louis, the Wehrenberg Theater chain pays particular attention to appealing to older customers. They turn up the heat and they turn up the *sound*. No one wants to admit that they cannot hear well, but loud, high-pitched voices are offensive and frequently incomprehensible to older patients. In dealing with them, the doctor should remember to

1. speak slowly
2. speak in a deep voice
3. look straight at the patient

Make It Clear

I'm a great Tom Peters fan, and I particularly enjoyed a videotape he made pointing out problems in communication. He tells about leaving the Rafael Hotel in Chicago with the doorman's instruction to turn at the "watertower." The watertower in Chicago doesn't look anything like the watertower in most small towns, so you can guess what happened. In his book, *Thriving on Chaos*, Peters put it succinctly (Peters 1987): You have to listen constantly. Listening, he says, means paying attention. It isn't just a matter of the patient's "compliance" about which we hear so much. Like the restaurant I mentioned earlier, it is a matter of attention to details. Older patients want, can afford, and expect competent eye care. If they do not like the *other* things about your office, they simply will not return.

Communicating with them means not only expressing yourself clearly but tailoring your message to the needs, concerns, temperament, and even vocabulary of the patient. One-on-one communication calls for somewhat different strategies and skills than you would use in preparing printed material, but the same principle applies. When you prepare any document—a brochure, correspondence, or newsletter—start with a specific goal. Always take a positive approach and be sure that your words communicate your personal enthusiasm to the patient. Don't forget the aesthetics. Include some tailored images that are light and friendly and match your desire for service to the older patient's needs. Benefits, benefits, benefits!

6

□ □ □
□ □ □
□ □ □

Problem-Solving

It was 1960, John Kennedy was wrapping up his problems with Richard Nixon, and a lot of new contact lens wearers were facing problems of their own. Then, as now, product promotion oversimplified lens-fitting procedures, and during that troubled period I learned a most valuable lesson: Most doctors don't want to see problem patients!

I'd be happy to take those cases off your hands, I told my colleagues, and they were just as anxious to make the referrals. Moreover, my reputation as an "expert," thus established, brought in many more. With people like that, who cared about competition?

About 10 years later, L.L. Weed, M.D., added some formality and system to basic health examinations (Weed 1971). Called SOAP, his widely used acronym in medical record keeping simply follows a logical order, accumulating data and taking appropriate measures based upon its significance. Subjective, Objective, Assessment, and Plan—it's equally valuable applied to contact lenses.

Accurate statistics are rare, but a little arithmetic indicates the number of persons wearing contacts is scarcely growing each year. It follows that there must be nearly as many people dropping out as there are beginners. Somewhere between 15 and 20 million Americans are evidently having trouble with their lenses.

In describing fitting procedures, or patient management, it fits our convenience to think of patients as new to the practice or even new to contact lens wear. When we speak of a particular clinical or management technique, we are likely to act as though the practitioner is beginning afresh each time and has never before encountered this individual patient.

In actuality, of course, the opposite is true. In any established practice the vast majority of patients is returning for continuing care and, more specifically, with some particular problem. Even more significant is the number of people who have previously worn lenses and are now in the process of changing doctors. When I was in practice, 90% of the new patients in our office had worn contacts at some time or another, and there is no reason to believe that ratio would be any lower today.

This perspective makes it clear that the majority is seeking something more than simply being able to see without glasses. That fact alone is scarcely noteworthy, but its impact on established management procedures is becoming increasingly evident.

Solving Problems in General

When George and Alec Gallup wrote *The Great American Success Story*, a book based on a survey of 1500 successful people, they listed common sense as the most common characteristic of those who reached the top of the ladder (Gallup and Gallup 1986). Successful people can make sound judgments on the everyday affairs of life and brush away extraneous, irrelevant thoughts and ideas to get to the core of what matters.

Without being specific, let's talk about reaching solutions of any kind. How adept are you at solving problems? Do you approach challenges with a sense of fun and excitement or with genuine apprehension? Pay the bills, stop smoking, get the kids into college—life could be so much simpler, right? Wrong! The process never ends. Successful living, like successful contact lens practice, is the direct result of our ability to creatively meet and solve the never-ending and perplexing matters we encounter.

I suppose if there is any primary rule, it must surely be to accurately assess and define a situation before rushing into it. Be certain that you know what you are trying to accomplish before taking that first step, lest you find yourself wasting a lot of precious time and energy. Consider every possible solution no matter how unlikely it may seem at first. Get into unrestrained possibility thinking. Before rejecting any idea (no matter how ridiculous or absurd), pause long enough to evaluate it fairly with the benefit of a positive open mind. It is easy to fall into a rut and accept things as true simply because we have failed to question the validity and accuracy of some basic data. I won't belabor the point. Just let problem-solving become habitual.

You Are Not Alone

People in trouble take more time. They return more often for longer visits in your office. This places greater emphasis on the importance of increasing your volume without expanding hours and, hopefully, without reducing service. More efficient management includes assignment of responsibility to ancilliary personnel, and delegation of such responsibility is contingent upon assurance that tests will be efficaciously completed. In other words, your technicians must be good problem-solvers, too.

The problem-oriented practice is dominated by the time-worn plea "Don't bring me problems, bring me solutions." From your patient's first call to your receptionist's greeting to the history to the examination, every act has to be directed toward identification. Once stated and assessed, then, full attention goes toward the solution. And, before the patient can leave, a single question must bar the way: *Has the problem been solved?*

Training People to Think

Judgment cannot be taught. But, if recognition of a problem followed to its ultimate solution is the epitome of a problem-oriented practice, the key word is *really* (Bredell 1984). Does a genuine problem *really* exist? Do we *really* know what it is, and if one is indeed present, how serious is it?

Would the patient go back to glasses? Are the new lenses better than the old ones? Is it just conversation or a ploy for attention? Does the problem involve one eye or two? (Unilateral problems deserve more attention.) What happens when the lenses are reversed? Did inspection of the lenses reveal a flaw in one or the other? Can the condition be eliminated with a diagnostic lens? How old are the materials, etc.?

Your technician should understand the onset of a problem. It may be related to other factors, especially compliance with instructions. How does a current lens vary from the original specifications? Have there been refractive or physical changes? Does the study of case records indicate that this or a similar condition existed before? Without a genuine and thorough understanding of the problem, there is little likelihood that you or your aide will accidently arrive at any workable solution.

I used to ask the AC/DC questions: Is it *adaptive* or *correctable* (AC)? If it is adaptive, the patient should be so advised and action held to a minimum. If the problem is correctable, appropriate measures must be taken at once.

Is the problem *dormant* or *critical* (DC)? Determining what is dormant, of course, is largely a matter of professional judgment. Limbal loops, tarsal papillae observed over an extended period of time, pingueculi, and other minor deviations from the norm may often be nearly meaningless. Attempted correction can sometimes create a whole series of new problems. A condition viewed as critical, on the other hand, demands positive action.

The Three Fs

Is it *fixable?* Is action *feasible?* Will it be *financially* sound—this is the true test of judgment.

A matter may be fixable, a quarter diopter of residual astigmatism for example, but prescribing a toric lens would scarcely be feasible. The third F, financially sound, is entirely practical. Who pays? In clinical practice, theory must be tempered by practical economic considerations.

Problem-Oriented Record Keeping

With the probable exception of Skeffington's standard 21-point examination, optometric record keeping has largely been a matter of personal preference. The diversity is nowhere more apparent than in the filing of case information for contact lens patients. I've asked a good many questions of audiences during my practice management lectures, and the responses generally indicate that only a few are using printed records designed or supplied by someone outside of their own offices. One might thus assume that we are wasting a lot of valuable time reinventing and duplicating record systems. Therefore, I am not suggesting you make any major changes, except in the way you look at the situation.

Not too many years ago I mailed a questionnaire to a significant sampling of optometrists and found that the information gathered in each office is apparently quite similar, but the order of presentation is hopelessly varied (Koetting 1983). Almost 85% designed their own forms, and a good many simply recorded contact lens information on blank cards. In fact, more than half kept contact lens information in a file separate from the patient's health and vision history. I suppose I am bringing this up only to explain why I won't be talking about a specific record style; however, there is certain common information that must be recorded.

The Problem-Oriented Entry Point

No examination is performed without a reason. If a patient does not make a clear statement, the purpose must evidently be determined through a series of questions or by some experienced assumptions. The first item is, logically, *the purpose of the examination:* Why has the patient come to your office? (Figure 6.1). So simple, yet rarely given the attention it deserves.

This original motivation may ultimately lead to something entirely different, but at the start, each patient has a goal. Perhaps the patient wants no more than an examination, or expects to replace a lens, or have an uncomfortable condition remedied by a simple adjustment. Ask! When the patient expects to be fitted with a new lens, the preference of type is important, although it ought not to be binding upon the doctor. A rigid lens, soft lens, extended wear, disposable, or whatever—at the conclusion of your exam and before advising the patient, these preferences have to be considered.

Don't Assume Baseline Data

Before any action becomes appropriate, a collection of baseline data is essential. Your technician may record lens position and movement

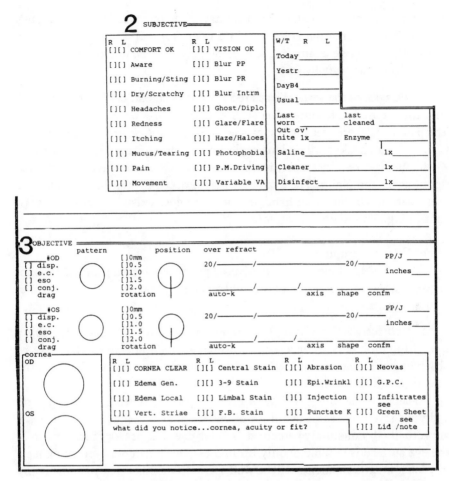

Figure 6.1 Subjective and objective questions to ask. Why is the patient in your office? A quick checklist helps your assistant sum up the information and provides a quick list of signs and symptoms.

and relationship of the lens edge to surrounding tissue. In the case of a soft lens, the possibility of blood-vessel impingement and conjunctival drag is noted. For rigid lenses (and if desired with soft lenses using large molecular dye), fluorescein patterns are drawn. Acuity, over-refraction, and best VA are shown and keratometry recorded. A patient's lens-wearing habits are included with the number of hours the lenses were worn today, yesterday, and the day before, etc. It is only human nature for patients to report what they think we want to hear. Don't settle for easy answers. Removal and care procedures should be recorded, and the results of laboratory inspection—radiuscope, surface quality, etc. — noted when lenses have been removed from the patient's cornea. This information is intended for reference and is, to some extent, a part of the objective exam, but it does not involve the doctor. Now comes the thinking part step-by-step.

1. *Purpose of the visit.* Why is the patient in the office? There are really only three possibilities following an initial visit: (a) A progress examination (the patient is there, because he or she thinks, or the doctor advised, that it is time for a checkup), (b) a lens replacement, or (c) some problem exists.

In the first two instances, further case history is unnecessary if the patient has no complaint. The examiner may proceed to step #3, the objective examination. On the other hand, if a problem does exist, it is either new or continuing. The interrogation follows.

Example
Mrs. Jones is a well-adapted presbyope wearing an RGP monovision correction. She has not been scheduled for a routine visit at this time. "I just want my left lens polished" is recorded as the purpose of her visit.

2. *Subjective.* What does the patient have to say? What are the subjective vision problems (as opposed to lowered acuity and matters that may be observed but are not annoying)? How about comfort? In short, what does the *patient* think is wrong?

In-depth questioning will be of great help here. When a patient reports a "drying" sensation, some definitive discussion may reveal whether the lenses are actually dry or simply perceived as being dry. The sensory mechanism of the eye surface is capable of only limited response. Almost everything feels "dry." A few extra moments will be well spent. Remember that we must *really* understand the patient.

Vision problems related to contact lenses are rarely confined to acuity. Night driving, glare and flare, lens movement, photophobia, haze, and ghost images are considered relative to other signs and symptoms. A checklist will simplify the procedure by destroying one's temptation to write down everything that comes to the patient's mind.

Example
Why did Mrs. Jones only want the left lens polished? Because that is her near-seeing eye and she is having some trouble reading. All of the time? No, she says, actually the vision isn't quite so bad on occasion, but it comes and goes, and, besides, there is some annoying lid sensation when she blinks.

Baseline information notes that she has a new job and is now doing sustained near-work. It is also noted, however, that there is no change in her lens power requirements.

3. *Objective.* What did *you* observe? Now it's your turn. How do the corneas look? What about the lids and conjunctiva? What do you think of the lens position, movement, and surface condition? If everything looks all right, say so and go to step #8. If it does not, record the information—this is the place for comments and observations.

Example

Mrs. Jones' slit lamp exam reveals some light punctate limbal staining that had not previously been noted at about 8 o'clock O.S. Further reference to baseline information shows no serious deviation from established wearing habits. Also, the left lens positions high on the cornea and moves up more than the right during blinking.

4. *Assessment.* What do you think is wrong? What caused this problem? *How* did it cause the problem? Now is the time for you and/or your technician to stop and give the matter some serious thought (Figure 6.2). If the baseline information and collected data are adequate, the cause should be clear. If not, further testing is indicated.

A subjective refraction or use of trial lenses may provide the necessary clues. Additional history also may reveal clues to *really* understanding the complaint.

WHAT IS REALLY THE PROBLEM? WHAT CAUSED IT? HOW?_____

4 _____

_____

===
WHAT WILL CORRECT THE PROBLEM? HOW?_____

5 _____

_____

===
ACTION and Lab Instructions (What Did We Do?)_____

6 _____

_____

===
NEXT VISIT (If No Improvement):_____

7 _____

_____

===
WHAT WAS THE PATIENT TOLD?_____

8 _____

Dismiss: Problem Solved?:_

Figure 6.2 Assessment, plan, and where to go from here. Step-by-step through the solution: What is really the problem, what caused it, and how? What can we do about it? What did we do, and what if that doesn't work? What was the patient told? If the problem hasn't been solved, be prepared to start over.

"Assessment," as used here, is a great deal more than an overview. It must indicate, in the fewest possible words, the problem's underlying cause without restating the signs and symptoms. "Hypoxia from steep lens" or "coated lens adheres to lid, vision varies with movement, etc." tells the whole story. Obviously, two or more problems may coexist, so each should be noted in the fewest possible words.

Example
Further reference to baseline information shows Mrs. Jones' left lens has warped and is flat. Your assessment reads, "O.S. lens warped flat, moves up, blur from lower edge."

5. *Plan.* Now, what do you think will correct the problem and how? If the matter has been properly assessed and described, the plan ought to be obvious. The more time spent assessing the problem, the easier its solution. You might note: "Assessment: Lens tight. Plan: Open secondary curve or replace with flatter lens." The plan need not be specific and may include more than one alternative. Here we like to consider the "3 Fs."

Example
In Mrs. Jones' case it is obvious the lens must be replaced. There also is some possibility that she would be better served by refitting with a bifocal, but that would not be a *feasible* suggestion for a person who "wanted a lens polished." The plan: replace lens O.S.

6. *Action.* What did you do? Write it down. How was the plan (or plans) executed? This is the detailed information for future reference. Alterations in the lens specifications, information involving exchange of materials, or even patient instructions must be recorded.

Example
Mrs. Jones' lens was replaced.

7. *Next visit.* What will you do next if this doesn't work? Proper documentation will prevent future frustration and will save minutes or hours later on. Future strategy is usually best planned when data are fresh and the patient is physically present. A few seconds spent looking over alternate solutions provide a perfect springboard into the next visit.

Example
For Mrs. Jones, if problems continue (1) unbalanced readers over for use on the job, (2) refit B.F. later.

8. *What was the patient told?* Far more than a face-saving device, a record of the exact parting words are precious to doctor and patient alike. "Could

you tell me again what the doctor said I should do about this problem?" is a pretty common request in every office. Thousands of arguments and lawsuits support the advantage of writing down advice and directions to the patient. Many of the more common instructions can be represented in a checklist for standardization and easy reference.

Example

And now, what was Mrs. Jones told? (1) We will give you an Rx for supplementary reading glasses if your problem continues. (2) You may have to be refitted with bifocals later. (3) Use lubricating drops qqh for the next 3 days.

That Very Important Bottom Line

Has the problem been solved? The question is literally the bottom line, and the answer is never "No."

Every visit must reach a conclusion. That is not to imply immediate or unqualified success in patient handling, but time to adapt or a return to glasses are legitimate conclusions. No case can be ended by hoping the problem will go away.

The foregoing does not imply that the SOAP approach is foolproof. It is by no means a substitute for clinical competence, but facing a future patient population composed almost entirely of dissatisfied lens wearers will be a whole lot easier with some organization.

Whatever Happened to Common Sense?

You don't often hear this expression anymore. Perhaps when I say "common sense," I'm dating myself and the advice I want to include here. This is, after all, a "management" book, so you won't find many specific remedial measures, even in these words about problem-solving. Common sense implies good practical judgment. You are a professional. You have a license and a clinical background. These are our tools, but we have all seen colleagues without enough common sense to make them work.

A generation ago, using technicians in a contact lens practice was considered pretty avant-garde. Most doctors were willing to let the "girls" type letters and make trips out for coffee, but when it came to patient handling, these assistants demanded direct supervision. When our office began to leave a major portion of the decision-making process in their hands, we faced two serious challenges. First, I couldn't afford to let anyone make a mistake. Second, there had to be some guidelines. The following set of rules dates back to 1972, but I wouldn't change them today.

□ □ □ □ □ "Don'ts" for Technicians

- act unless you are *sure* it will help
- stop working to talk
- forget to read the record
- keep others waiting by spending more than the allotted time with any patient
- make adjustments on the basis of theory alone
- order anything without evaluating trial lenses first
- open vials or make insignificant changes without due process of thought

Looking back, these "don'ts" sound a bit high-handed, although the common-sense message boils down to a simple admonition: Please don't waste time doing anything without a good reason. I've visited the offices of many, many colleagues and all too often heard them say, "Well, let's just try another lens and see if that works any better." I don't think we would ordinarily call that problem-solving.

Rule Out Pathology

From *Acanthamoeba* to *Zepherin*, we could devote at least a volume to red eyes. There are lots of causes, and, hopefully, you know what they are. Contact lenses often traumatize a cornea, leaving the way open for invasion by pathogens, and I certainly don't mean to put down the importance of these problems. We've heard a great deal about patient compliance, and that's important, too.

Most of us don't stick to our diets, and others who know they shouldn't, continue to smoke. Even in the face of life-threatening conditions, we are told that many people don't take proper medication. Ferreting out those who don't comply with contact lens instructions offers quite a challenge.

Solving the noncompliers problem involves two considerations. First, we must educate patients and get cooperation. But, secondly, if we expect to continue making a living in the field, we must stop scaring them to death. A calm, intelligent approach to the risks involved should be sufficient. No one would argue against the significance of informed consent, but most current literature would have us believe that covering our backsides is more important than doing a good job. The very low incidence of serious trouble, considering the 20 million contact lens wearers (most of whom aren't following the rules anyway), indicates that taking time to instruct and encourage patients is a lot more important—and a whole lot better for the practice—than making them read and sign a list of horrible possibilities. Communicating with patients will be discussed elsewhere, but in the context of problem-solving, it may involve informed consent.

☐ ☐ ☐ ☐ ☐ Informed Consent Requirements

- a description of the eye problem
- your proposed treatment
- any risks associated with that treatment
- alternative treatments (including doing nothing)
- any risks associated with the alternatives

Malpractice

The inclusion of comments on malpractice insurance at this point will be limited to the suggestion that you obtain adequate coverage and relax. Take a hypothetical worst-case scenario and you'll probably find it is the insurance carrier that really needs to worry. This is a serious matter, and one that ought never be taken lightly, but if the cost of insurance is actually prohibitive, you probably shouldn't stay in practice. Otherwise, do the best you can and try not to let concerns with litigation cloud your judgment.

We really don't know how many O.D.s are in legal trouble, but the number must be very small compared to other professions. Based on insurance rates, optometrists are certainly doing far better than M.D.s. Friendly, informative conversation during and following a contact lens fitting is your best defense against litigation. Keep in mind that patients don't sue people they like.

Materials Versus Common Sense

I'm appalled by the idea that a little extra oxygen going through a piece of plastic is supposed to be effective in eliminating almost every contact lens discomfort known to man. Perhaps educators and writers are becoming more realistic, but manufacturers would still have us believe that lens movement, edge standoff, thickness, weight, and a dozen other considerations are secondary to DK. I have nothing against RGP (Rigid Gas Permeable) contact lenses, except to be alarmed by the idea that changing materials will solve problems which are almost totally a matter of physical construction. Even more distressing is the situation wherein some lucky clinician replaces an ill-fitted lens with one made of some other material. And, if the comfort problem is resolved in some manner, credit is given to the plastic instead of the design. Once again, let's look for the real cause.

☐ ☐ ☐ ☐ ☐ Contact Lens Problems, One Eye

- switch lenses
- check lens specifications

- try the patient's old lenses
- check the old lenses again
- put on a trial lens
- study lens age
- see two-eye problem list
- think

☐ ☐ ☐ ☐ ☐ **Contact Lens Problems, Two Eyes**

- note onset of problem
- look at *original* specifications
- study *all* previous trial lenses
- study *all* previous changes
- think

Your Very Best Trial Lens

Serious consideration goes to the first suggestion under "one-eye problems." When I was in practice, it sometimes seemed that hardly a day went by without a call from some other O.D. wishing to discuss a case. More often than not, the conversation involved someone who was having trouble with only one eye. "The right lens has been OK from the beginning," the story would usually begin, "but I've tried everything on the left"—thick lens, thin lens, bitoric, soft, RGP, you name it. Nothing seemed to work on that left eye. "Did you try the right lens?" I would usually ask, and I'll bet you can guess the answer.

It seems so obvious. If a patient has a lens that works on one eye, why not try it on the other eye? Just ordering one lens, made to what are supposed to be the same specifications, doesn't prove a thing.

When patients called our office with comfort problems involving only one eye, our assistants asked two fundamental questions: Is the eye uncomfortable when your contacts are off? Does the lens feel bad if you put it on the other eye? When a problem can be associated with one lens, assessment is so much simpler.

Loose Lenses

This isn't supposed to be a clinical text, but my problem-solving experience with rigid lenses has shown one error to be so common it must be singled out for discussion. All hard lenses, particularly RGP, tend to warp. And when they do, remedial action is often counterproductive.

If warpage results in a slight toricity, and the resultant residual astigmatism is not serious, don't touch it! Such lenses are often very comfortable, but bear in mind, you will have plenty of questions to answer when the time comes for its replacement. Warped lenses often attach to the upper lid and ride high; we may even think this positioning is desirable. However, movement can be very annoying and patients are often upset by the inconsistent vision involved. Don't ever assume that RGP specifications are a constant.

Then there is the matter of paracentral steepening. This condition is not easily explained. It is generally accepted that a hard lens absorbs small amounts of water when kept in an aqueous environment and that this absorption is accompanied by a measurable amount of flattening. For many years we have known that concave lenses with the thinnest centers exhibit the greatest change. Because a lens tends to flatten in ratio to its thickness, then, it must be speculated that the maximum flattening will occur in the thinner center of a concave lens and that its periphery will remain more or less stable.

If the diameter of a lens does not increase appreciably, one of two things will likely follow hydration: the lens may become toric or the paracentral area of the optic zone will be altered. This will result in a "buckling" process. The change that is found when one presses on a beach ball, for example, shows how the radius of the surface immediately surrounding the flattened area will be decreased. Because the overall diameter cannot increase, the curvature of adjacent material must change to compensate for the longer arc and shorter sagitta. In other words, some other portion of a flattening lens will become steeper!

Thus, a high-minus contact lens that flattens upon hydration will typically produce some "tight" lens symptoms, because the paracentral area has actually adopted a steeper radius of curvature while allowing for expansion of the thinner middle portion. Observation of this phenomenon is impossible when a lens curve is measured with a standard radiuscope or keratometer, because those instruments do not include the affected area. A practical clinical application of the foregoing can be summed up in a simple rule: When a high-minus rigid lens causes discomfort or corneal insult, and measurement of the base curve indicates that it has flattened, grinding out the secondary area may be wiser than discarding it or remaking the lens to its original specifications.

Low-Vision Patients: A Forgotten Group

The problem-oriented practice is, for all practical purposes, synonymous with use of specialty lenses. I suggest that the fitting of low-vision patients can very well be included in the services offered.

People are living longer. Everyone knows that, and if you have attended any optical trade shows recently, you also know that a great deal of attention is being focused on the visual infirmities of old age. The ever-increasing number of low-vision-aid suppliers is testimony enough that these problems are getting some attention.

Why Contact Lenses?

Techniques for the fitting of contact lenses involving special designs are quite adequately covered in many other books and will not be repeated here. In the management of certain conditions, keratoconus for example, vision may be improved with contacts to such a degree that a patient may be totally removed from the low-vision category.

There is a small but impressive number of persons for whom contact lenses produce acuity vastly improved over that obtained with spectacles. The covering of scarred or irregular corneas, increased image size in myopia, elimination of aniseikonia in aphakia, the control of high astigmatism, and reduced nystagmus represent areas where contacts have traditionally been used to advantage. Less common, but sometimes spectacularly effective, is the Galilean telescope, a combination of contact lenses and spectacles. A variety of cosmetic and high-add lenses also work once in a while, but only when the practitioner is willing to try.

Irregular Corneas

RGP contact lenses, by providing a regular refractive surface to replace an irregular cornea, produce greatly improved visual acuity. Historically, there has been suggestions that contacts either stop or slow the progression of keratoconus, although documentation is sketchy, and improved vision remains the best reason for their use. Apical bearing or clearance techniques remain controversial and will not be dealt with here, except to point out that the cornea of a keratoconus patient is not an initially healthy one, so the tissue must be watched closely for adverse changes during lens wear.

Small or moderate degrees of keratoconus may sometimes be corrected with soft contact lenses, producing only minimal amounts of residual refractive error that can occasionally be corrected with spectacles. The virtues of combining flexible and rigid contacts in a "piggyback" system have been extolled for years, although the obvious scarcity of satisfied wearers lends no testimony to the method's acceptance.

A soft carrier lens is applied in the conventional manner, incorporating a large optic zone so that the rigid lens does not extend beyond the edge of the front bevel. A thin plano bandage lens about .10 mm flatter and about .50 mm larger in diameter than might ordinarily be used will generally work quite well. The final specifications of the rigid lens are determined through the use of diagnostic lenses. Lid irritation is reduced by taking care to eliminate edge standoff.

Hard and soft lenses function in much the same manner to provide a regular refracting surface for a damaged cornea or postoperatively in cases of penetrating keratoplasty. Because injuries often involve corneal opacity, aniridia, or an irregular pupil, a cosmetic lens also may be employed to advantage. Partial masking is easily obtained with an opaque cosmetic tint.

A very high myope is classically recognized as a good candidate for contact lenses. Spectacles produce minification (compared to unaided vision) in myopia, and the amount may be greatly reduced by switching to contacts. Thus, relative to a myopic spectacle correction, the contact lens produces a magnified image on the retina. A contact correction for a 15.00-diopter myope, for example, would produce a 19.5% larger image than spectacles at a vertex distance of 13 mm. As a general rule, practitioners might expect an increase of about 1% retinal image size for each diopter of myopia when a patient converts from glasses. The stable, well-centered lens also enhances vision by eliminating peripheral distortion and prismatic effects usually encountered with thick eyeglasses. It should be noted, unfortunately, that this is not always to the advantage of a high myope. More accommodation is required to focus this eye-lens optical system for near distances when the myope is corrected with contact lenses than when that patient uses spectacles. Moreover, many high myopes take advantage of their natural vision by reading at a very close distance with spectacles removed.

Emotional Problems

As obvious as it may seem, practitioners tend to overlook the *psychological* advantage of contact lenses. Because a myopic condition generally begins early in life and produces changes in vision and lenses, the patient is often emotionally traumatized by this affliction. The symbolic significance of being able to see without glasses may be the most important single thing that happens to a high myope.

Aphakia

For the partly sighted aphakic, image size becomes a more serious consideration and challenge to the clinician. A low-vision aphake (without an IOL) enjoys the magnification accidently available through the use of spectacle lenses. Binocularity may or may not be perceived as an improvement over glasses.

Nystagmus

Several authors have reported on cases of nystagmus that have been significantly reduced and visual acuity enhanced by the use of contacts.

It has been speculated that nystagmus produced by a visual cause may be reduced or eliminated if lenses can effectively correct that visual defect. If the refractive correction can be incorporated into a soft lens, the benefit to the patient is evidently greater.

Telescopes

The idea of using a contact lens as the eyepiece of a Galilean telescope has been reported in the literature since 1939. William Ludlam designed a scleral, and after that a soft lens, system with high minus power for the eyepiece and strong convex spectacles as the objective. His work has served as the basis for all modern contact lens–telescope systems. Ludlam's original specification involved – 40.00-D contact lens and a + 26.00-D spectacle lens to produce a 1.5× magnification at a vertex distance of 13 mm.

With the development of more consistent and better soft contact lenses, the system is finding wider acceptance. – 30.00-D soft lenses are available from several laboratories. + 20.00-D aspheric spectacle lenses provide a much wider field and can be fabricated to include toric components for correction of the residual astigmatism so often encountered with hydrogels. Soft lenses, even in such high powers, are quite acceptable to most persons during the first trial fitting. A range of several base curves (preferably in pairs) ought to be available in the practitioner's office in addition to finished + 20.00-D spectacles in a variety of sizes and common PD. A more sophisticated system involves combining the contact with a specially designed bioptic spectacle.

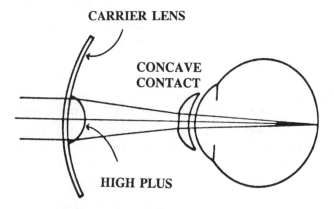

CARRIER LENS

CONCAVE
CONTACT

HIGH PLUS

Figure 6.3 The telecon system. Management of low vision has become increasingly important in optometric practice. Contact lenses can be useful in a variety of ways.

Minification

The use of a reverse Galilean telescope to enlarge the object field for those patients having constricted fields but good visual acuity has been tried on occasion (Figure 6.3). Combining a strong convex contact lens with a concave spectacle correction has generally proved unworkable, because the thick and heavy contact will not stay in position and the high-concave spectacle correction causes a counterproductive field limitation.

Albinism

The photophobia that accompanies a lack of pigmentation can be annoying and even painful in extreme cases. Additionally, children may experience great psychological trauma as a result of "pink eyes." A special-order opaque lens will reduce unwanted light passing through the sclera, but these patients are generally helped by *any* device that reduces the impact of glare. A heavily tinted conventional corneal lens will often provide appreciable relief.

Now What?

We are all problem-solvers. But, a giant wave of mediocrity is sweeping over what was once a very technically oriented field. The best defense against such change is your personal reputation for meeting challenges. After all, most doctors don't want to see problem patients.

7

Staffing a Practice for Successful Marketing

Who talks to your patients more than you do? Darned near everyone on your staff, that's who!

As far as patients are concerned, your employees *are* your office. Furthermore, we all know that the road to genuine efficiency is paved with delegation, even though most of us are dragged onto it, kicking and screaming, in a futile effort to maintain what we perceive to be total control. Economist Robert B. Nelson (Nelson 1988) provides a list of the most common excuses for not delegating in corporate management, proving, I suppose, it's a small world. Doesn't this sound familiar?

Excuses for Not Delegating

1. My staff lacks experience.
2. It takes more time to explain than to do the job myself.
3. A mistake by one of my technicians could be costly.
4. My patients will pay more attention to me.
5. There are just some things I shouldn't delegate to anyone.
6. My staff lacks the overall knowledge necessary to make proper decisions.
7. They are already too busy.
8. They just aren't ready to accept more responsibility.
9. I'm concerned about lack of control when I delegate.
10. I enjoy keeping busy and making my own decisions.

Excuses, excuses! Let's take a closer look at them.

- If your staff lacks experience, and it takes more time than you have to explain things, you have at least three alternatives: train them yourself, send them to meetings or courses, or hire better-trained people. In any event, you need help.

- Mistakes *are* costly, and they can be avoided by heeding the foregoing advice.
- Patients will usually accept matters of policy from a staff member when they might not take it from the doctor. Would you be comfortable, for example, saying "cash in advance" to your next-door neighbor or your wife's cousin?
- There certainly are some things you shouldn't delegate, but far fewer than you might imagine. You will be surprised how people rise to responsibility, and how office morale will go up, when you begin to delegate.
- If your staff is already too busy, it won't be long before *you* will be too busy to help them. Then what?

During the last 10 years, optometrists have begun to view the use of lay assistants as a real hope for quality vision care on an overpopulated horizon. This efficiency ultimately benefits the patient, of course, but the rewards are not one-sided. Providing better service simply means that patients will not be forced to seek it elsewhere, and more productive use of professional time is nearly synonymous with a profitable bottom line.

We all know there are doctors who allot 10 minutes or so to each office visit, yet give the impression of having all of the time in the world to devote to every patient. Then there are those who can keep someone in the office for an hour and still leave the patient feeling there wasn't enough time to do the job right. It is largely a matter of attitude.

When the optometrist has confidence in the office staff and subtly conveys this faith to the patient, especially by avoiding disagreements within earshot and occasionally complimenting the technician or calling attention to a prudent decision, the acceptance is contagious. Furthermore, taking a few seconds to review a case record while your patient watches is an absolute must.

Where to Draw the Line

Drawing a distinctive line between "doctor skills" and "technician skills" would, at best, be a seriously controversial task. Some things, like examination of the fundus, are certainly best accomplished by the doctor, but other things (and this is the area we are inclined to overlook) like recording test results or placing a contact lens on a patient's eye, are much better left to someone else. In its briefest form, patients expect, and ethics demand, that the optometrist perform those acts that involve professional judgment and licensure and are beyond the training of a technician. With a very few exceptions, the paraprofessional can work to a level that is limited only by the amount of responsibility the boss wishes to assume. Contact lens fitting probably offers the maximum opportunity for utilization of technical personnel because that task and many others are actually better performed by paraprofessionals.

It is our purpose here to deal with duties directly related to contact lenses. The receptionist, secretary, bookkeeper, porter, and related jobs will be disregarded for the moment. Two other non-contact lens–related occupations, executive assistant and refracting assistant, however, are worthy of special attention.

The Administrative/Executive Assistant

Managing any successful practice requires a combination of professional competence and administrative ability. During the early years of solo practice, most doctors can perform both tasks. If they handle them efficiently, the practice will grow so that they will soon be seeing patients to the limit of their physical capabilities (Koetting 1981).

At that point, the doctor seeks aid and most often attempts employment of, or association with, another optometrist, almost invariably forgetting that patients want to see the founder of the practice. Hiring an executive assistant is often much wiser. Building a healthy practice by seeing more patients during time that might be spent on management is a major advantage. But, there are certainly others. Reduced likelihood of personality clashes; single, unquestioned leadership; and simplicity in terminating the relationship are pretty good for a start. Furthermore, most optometrists are actually very poor administrators. A good executive will provide a practical, tough nonprofessional point of view that ought to supplement the doctor's experience with a much wider knowledge of office procedures.

A few O.D.s have been fortunate enough to find such capable individuals at the very moment the practice had grown enough to justify employment of an executive. However, most are unhappily saddled with acceptance of unqualified persons who were originally hired without management capabilities. When promoting from the ranks is absolutely impossible, the time-consuming procedure of hiring and training a stranger is the only alternative.

Wearing Two Hats

Let's face it, every one of us has two jobs, and the professional personality seems to get tired first. Maybe it's because we *have* to practice optometry, it is our chosen career. It's getting up and going to work every day. It is talking to patients we would sometimes rather not see or listening to complaints we would rather not hear. Practicing optometry seems like drudgery because that's our job.

The other job seems like fun. Being an executive is a reward. Making decisions and spending money, hiring people, buying equipment, dallying with salespeople, making long-distance phone calls with feet on the desk, or keeping a bottle of Chardonnay in your private refrigerator—these things are fun! This is the "executive life," and the job gets bigger and more prestigious as the practice grows. Frankly, most of us think the executive life is our reward and really want more of it. That is why busy O.D.s hope to find another optometrist who will see the patient while leaving the fun and games to them. When it comes time to seek more help, it is tough to realize that it is the administrative tasks that ought to be delegated.

I also noticed another advantage long ago: unquestioned leadership. A single doctor heading any organization is obviously in charge. The fewer professionals in the office, the less conflict and reduced likelihood of personality conflicts. Besides, in seeking an associate, how many have real clerical or accounting experience? How many, even if they were foolish enough to try, would type their own letters or do their own bookkeeping?

More Benefits

A good business administrator can provide a practical, tough nonprofessional point of view and can supplement your practical experience with a useful knowledge of office procedures. Naturally, we love expensive ego-boosting activities. Whether it is unnecessarily sophisticated equipment or membership in an organization that hasn't produced a patient in the last 5 years, we often tend to let emotions influence our purchases. That is not to say that an executive assistant will always be stoic, self-disciplined, and smarter than the doctor in money matters. Far from it. But, a good administrator working with an established budget can save us from our own mistakes by simply pointing out the wisdom, or lack of it, when some expenditure is contemplated. Sound judgment often involves time-consuming considerations, and this is an executive responsibility.

Purchases can often be better handled by a layman, and the same is certainly true of collections. A firm but pleasant voice explaining office policy will do more to hold down accounts receivable than almost anything else.

And speaking of money, there is another reason why you should hire an administrative assistant instead of an optometrist. An intelligent, loyal, capable, well-trained executive gives the O.D. all the extra time a doctor could acquire by taking in an associate for less than an optometrist's salary.

A third party can be quite valuable simply because of that person's disinterested position in office management. This is certainly true in the matter of hiring personnel, but particularly so in the rather sticky situation of interviewing patients or your personal friends for a position in the office. Such interviews are almost unavoidable in a small community where the doctor cannot conduct a personal interview or even say "no" without being mildly offensive to someone.

We've all faced it—"Do you have a job opening in your office? I've been thinking of going back to work again and would sure like to work with you." How comforting at times like these to politely "pass the buck" to your assistant by suggesting that the individual come in to complete an application for a possible interview later. You can explain that certain qualifications are involved and that you simply don't know which applications may already be under consideration.

This objective position is doubly helpful when discussion of other delicate matters is involved. A complaint on one of your aides or perhaps even your own work can be resolved without embarrassment. While your own forthright apology may often be the best answer, an explanation from your assistant can clarify matters without the appearance of whining. From accepting regrets for a late payment to facing the problems of a pregnant teenager, a well-trained and tactful administrator is usually more capable than the doctor. Of course, the ability to hold such things in confidence and the assurance of long-term employment are essential characteristics, as patients should never be encouraged to discuss personal matters with someone who is likely to be working in another office next week.

The Refracting Technician

Like the executive assistant, our refracting technicians were not a part of the contact lens team. The position requires a good background in optics and a general knowledge of the instruments involved in optometric data collection, so someone with formal education is preferable. The graduate of an optometric technician program has proven skill and a 2-year head start over an on-the-job–trained counterpart. It should be obvious in a smaller practice that the duties of one or more persons may be assumed by the same individual. The refracting technician, for example, may also serve as a chairside contact lens assistant. In a contact lens practice, formal education tends to bow to experience, particularly where lens application or interpretation of fitting characteristics is concerned.

Chairside Help

Accepting the premise that someone else handles clerical work is your office still leaves a lot to be accomplished by you and your instruments. There remains an enormous potential for paraprofessional aid that can increase efficiency, decrease overhead, and, in all likelihood, provide a better examination for the patient.

For some reason, most O.D.s like to record examination findings in their own hand. Due in part to a desire for accuracy, I suspect the real reason is more a matter of habit. At first, most of us just don't feel comfortable repeating examination results out loud. From the patient's point of view, however, nothing could be more impressive. The traditional "uh-huh" after every finding has summed up the layman's idea of doctor for centuries; however, it is much less acceptable than we would like to think.

Believe it or not, patients are glad to hear they have one diopter of habitual exophoria at distance, even if they don't have the vaguest notion of its significance. A disproportionate part of optometric refracting time is spent simply recording one's own activities. Why not let an assistant eliminate this waste, while thoroughly impressing the listener? And besides, you won't forget the numbers before you get them down on paper.

Contact Lens Instructor

As discounted materials including only bare-bones service are advertised with greater regularity, professionals are beginning to recognize that patient instruction is an integral part of contact lens service not to be taken lightly. Teaching the new lens wearer to handle them is a hallmark of the care that justifies higher fees, but the doctor's time will never be cheap enough to warrant the patience required. In fact, in a one-assistant office, tying up 100% of the ancillary personnel is almost as bad. Instruction takes time, and the instructor must be free of all interference until the task has been completed.

A part-time staffer with no other obligation is best suited, and such a person can be selected without serious consideration of any other qualifications. Many doctors feel that the instructor should be female, because women tend to relate better to men *and* women. Most men are somewhat embarrassed being taught by another male, tending to feign understanding when additional help is needed.

An instructor should be a mature person, preferably someone with teenage children. This maturity enables her to better relate to the older aphakic patient, to the adult patient, and, because she has children of her own, to teenagers. Furthermore, those with children away at school make ideal part-time employees. Because close contact is involved, the instructor must obviously be well groomed and exhibit excellent personal hygiene. These attributes are not limited to contact lens instruction, but are doubly important under what are usually tense and trying circumstances.

The idea of simultaneously fitting contact lenses for two, three, or four persons at one time, and subsequently instructing these patients as a group, will seem institutional or even commercial if you have not tried the method. During group instruction lens handling procedures are reinforced and slow learners reassured while they watch others perform the same task.

If psychologists are right in saying that information must be repeated five times before it is retained, you'll find welcome relief through the use of videotaped programs, also presented and operated by the instructor. Information is reinforced, reiterated, and, more importantly, presented with authority through the use of your own tapes or those supplied by lens and solution companies.

A Laboratory Technician

You can't learn to swim by reading a book about it, or so I've been told. And measuring an optic zone or polishing an edge requires genuine experience; no amount of professional or technical theory can be substituted. Thus, the ideal lab technician is chosen for dexterity and/or experience. This sets them somewhat apart from other paraprofessionals and makes recruitment much more difficult.

Additionally, the laboratory technician must nowadays combine the skills of inventory clerk and purchasing agent. Rigid lens expertise is nearly wasted in hydrogel practice, but bookkeeping ability is essential.

Training an unskilled laboratory technician takes a great deal of time. Fortunately, most commercial laboratories follow a pay scale sufficiently low that a ready supply of skilled technicians is available in large urban areas. In smaller communities, and in an office where technician's duties cover several other jobs, the O.D. has little choice but to educate his own.

In contact lens practice, as in general practice, most optometrists recognize that professional time cannot be justified in the laboratory. Nor is the patient well served when lenses must be removed for several days so that service can be performed in some outside lab.

□ □ □ □ □ Characteristics of the Best Lab Technicians

1. detail oriented
2. somewhat introverted because most of the job involves dealing with things instead of people
3. has sufficient communication skills to explain and apologize for problems
4. knows when to ask the doctor for information

Where To Start

Finding, interviewing, and hiring new employees is, if done right, one of the most important ways to achieve the goals of a successful practice. With the right team in place, you can move ahead quickly and effectively. Most doctors never give the interviewing and hiring process the time it deserves, and, to be perfectly honest, they really don't go about looking for prospects in a very effective manner.

It seems hard to believe today, but in my early years of practice I heard a prominent optometric management lecturer suggest that if you are satisfied with the service in a restaurant, you should hire the waitress. There *is* some validity in this rationale. It is easier to teach technical skills to persons with natural empathy and a pleasant personality than vice versa. Just the same, staffing your office unquestionably involves a lot more than raiding the fast-food counters. There are many, many books on the subject, and most of them will give you all of the basic information you will ever need. I suggest you buy and read one before your next staffing crisis. Meanwhile, I'll quote management expert Robert Heller, who says that hiring can never be an exact science. Just the same, he says employers must learn to rise above "gut feeling" to make really productive choices (Heller 1984).

In *Further Up the Organization*, Robert Townsend summarizes his hiring philosophy in a very practical way (Townsend 1984). To keep your office staff young and fit, he advises, don't hire anyone until your present employees are very busy. Besides, if a new person comes aboard in circumstances other than absolute necessity, people will wonder what is happening to the practice and whether their own jobs are in jeopardy.

The few times when I have been "burnt" in the process of hiring someone can generally be attributed to the same old mistake: haste. When you or your executive assistant interview someone, be careful about leaping to first impressions. From time to time say nothing and see what happens. Do a lot of listening.

The Good Old Classifieds

Management consultant and author Laura Sachs has a lot to say on the subject. Writing in *Optometric Management*, she offers some examples, good and bad (Sachs 1989).

Example
RECEPTIONIST
Optometric office. Full time. Experience preferred. Send resume: G-11, Journal.

Unless you are committed to being a receptionist and this is the only advertisement for such a position, you probably won't be very impressed. The ad
is unfortunately typical. It is also vague, impersonal, and lacks basic information such as salary, job benefits, and the employer's name. In short, it violates
just about every rule of effective classified advertising.

If times are tough, it might still generate a large number of responses. But,
as Sachs says, it is far better to run a good ad that attracts two or three
well-qualified applicants than a poor one that draws a hundred mediocre
respondents.

On the other hand, you really don't have to tell everything you know. Most
people now take for granted such standard employee benefits as personal days,
paid vacations, insurance, etc. Emphasize the things that make your office
different and attractive.

A few years ago I was inspired by a local cab company. On the classified
page, the advertisement covered several columns with a boldface, straightforward message somewhat as follows:

Example
WANTED
Good, clean-cut family men who are careful drivers, courteous, and concerned
for passengers. They must be honest, reliable, etc., etc., etc. Call Laclede Cab
Company, 123 4567.

The description certainly doesn't fit many cab drivers I know, but that
is not the point. We followed suit.

Example
THE KOETTING ASSOCIATES
The largest exclusive contact lens practice in the Midwest needs technicians
to serve its rapidly growing number of patients. If you are intelligent, per-
sonable, and genuinely interested in working with people, etc. etc. etc. When
people in St. Louis think of contact lenses, they think of The Koetting
Associates 863 0000.

Even if you are not inclined to take this approach, just remember that
every potential job applicant looks for short but catchy pieces of information—
part-time, western suburbs, near the interstate, pleasant surroundings, and,
of course, benefits, benefits, benefits. You can also save time by assigning a
secondary phone line to your advertisement. "Call between 9 and 11 A.M."
serves a couple of purposes: You will know what to expect when the phone
rings and, as a bonus, you can weed out people who can't follow instructions
when they call at 12:15.

My friend, Harriet Stein, well-known writer and lecturer, warns against acting in haste. When an aide suddenly takes leave for any reason, the ensuing panic can lead to hasty decisions based upon the fear that there is not enough time to screen and interview applicants from a newspaper ad. This leads to wondering whether the doctor should instead hire a friend or a patient.

"In all of my consulting experience," says Stein, "rarely have I witnessed a successful employee relationship when a friend was hired. A friend usually has a difficult time giving the doctor the respect required in an office environment. In addition, fellow employees feel that some favoritism may occur. Lastly and most importantly, the doctor feels uncomfortable giving directions or reprimanding. It's a recipe for failure (Stein 1990).

Don't Rush

Whenever there is a big hole in your practice where a key employee used to be, you will be justifiably tempted by a quick-fix solution: hire the first person who applies for the job.

Reconsider! Doctors who fall prey to the "warm body syndrome" often find themselves searching for yet another replacement a few months down the line. Finding the most suitable employee will take a few extra days, or even weeks, but careful hiring practices can save many dollars in turnover, training, and lost revenue. Like it or not, you must follow hiring procedures that best ferret out the right person for the job. Remember that using multiple interviewers provides a more complete picture of a candidate's capabilities, so if your executive is available to do some basic screening, talk to the best one or two yourself. This may also provide different insights on an applicant's personality and ability to fit in with the rest of your staff. Once the interviews are complete, you can compare notes and discuss impressions.

Beware of the "halo effect." This happens when an interviewer tells an applicant exactly what kind of person will be needed to fill the position, then asks the candidate to describe her- or himself. Surprise! The candidate's self-description — a parroting of the qualifications just listed by the interviewer — marks the applicant as the perfect person for the job. So what are you looking for? Pay close attention to ease of conversation and use of grammar. Be sure to start with an employment application, because that will contain the pertinent facts for your file and you can check handwriting and spelling. Make a special note of the condition of the person's clothes and hair. Look for someone who has a professional image, and notice how the person sits (interested and upright or slouched and indifferent).

References

Now comes another annoying and time-consuming obligation. According to one study, only 14% of employers answer candidly when asked to recommend former employees. Why? Fear of being sued among other things. Although the number of judgments against employers under such circumstances is really quite small, former employers can be awarded a great deal of money and most employers are afraid to say anything.

Ask for a phone or personal interview rather than a written recommendation. The previous employer will usually steer away from putting anything in writing, particularly if it is negative. A phone or personal interview will yield more telling results. People tend to be more candid when approached in person, and face-to-face meetings give you a chance to observe body language such as a raised eyebrow, heavy sigh, or uncertain expression beyond a favorable comment.

Don't ask directly about an applicant's weaknesses. Instead, say something like, "We have a training program in our office, what areas do you feel deserve special attention?"

A full third of all job applicants reportedly change their accomplishments in some way. Education, titles, job responsibility, or dates of employment and salaries are often inflated. When you think you have found a suitable person to fill the job, it is wise to be sure. By checking references thoroughly, you'll boost your chances of getting the right employee in your office.

The Interview

Of course you want to be right. Turnover is not only costly in itself but also can be crippling to a practice that is dependent on a small number of key people. Before a job applicant comes through your door, there are some steps that I have learned from staffing specialists that you can take to prevent hiring mistakes. The first critical factor, says John Curtis, vice president of the Orlando Consulting Group, is to look inward and understand your own practice. Gain an absolute clarity of what you want and how your new employee will fit into those parameters. Consider what combination of behavior and technical skills will work in your office.

Because interviewing skills are not taught in school Curtis advises before you learn to interview, first you have to realize that you don't know how. He further suggests reading books or taking courses on the subject. Consider, also, using the service of a professional recruiter or search firm. They can handle the initial screening and reference-checking to increase the chances that the applicant will perform according to expectations.

Dr. Miriam Hull of the Maitland, Florida, consulting firm of Hull, Levine, and Associates notes that the shocking part of turnover is that many times a person is let go or leaves not because they couldn't do the job but because they *wouldn't* do the job. Identifying the "want-tos" before a person is hired can make a difference.

As Robert Heller says, "Listen" (Heller 1984). It is important to find out what the applicant wants to ask. Are the questions frivolous and self-serving, or is there a professional level of interest in the job? People are anxious to know about such things as working hours. They do, after all, have personal lives, but there can be revealing nuances in all of this if you know how to spot them.

If the interviewee leaves you definitely uninterested, you may find it more comfortable not to talk about the bad news and handle it by letter—courtesy suggests that you do this within 2 weeks.

Keep interviews short. Abbreviated sessions can help you by allowing you to measure a candidate's sophistication, adaptability, and interpersonal skills. You can judge how well a candidate will fit into your practice by recognizing that very competent people—persons who have performed well for other doctors—may do miserably on your staff simply because they don't fit in. Avoid surprises by including a brief job description very early in the process.

□ □ □ □ □ Five Places to Look for New Employees

1. *Newspaper classified advertisements.* We have already talked about these. Write a good ad and make it stand out.

2. *Agencies.* This involves both employment and employee-leasing companies. It will cost you either way, but if you get a good return on your investment, who cares? On the other hand, you should be certain there will be no charge if the employee leaves or is terminated during some acceptable trial period.

3. *Optometric technician schools.* These should be the best possible source of talent, but rarely are. The graduates are often very young, not anxious to relocate, and may have unrealistic expectations. It's worth a call or letter though. There is no substitute for this level of training. (Some feel those who come from ophthalmic dispensing schools may be more mature, you will have to judge that for yourself.)

4. *Networking.* Talk to sales representatives and keep an eye on your competitors. Chain locations that are open 7 days a week or keep employees working until late in the evening can't hold them very long. Ophthalmic sales reps are in many offices and usually know when someone is not content.

5. *Keep your eyes open.* Friends usually make poor employees. Patients are much better, but firing a patient is risky if it doesn't work out. Some of my best staff members have come from the ranks of those wonderful, enthusiastic people who liked our office so well they wanted to work there.

And, although I scoffed at hiring waitresses, they are usually underpaid and overworked, as are people in retail sales of cosmetics, jewelry, or clothing. When you find someone who is well spoken and outgoing, training this "diamond-in-the-rough" may be a rewarding experience.

□ □ □ □ □ **Major Problems in Staffing**

I've asked a few optometrists who ought to know, just what they feel are the major staffing problems. Here is the list:

1. Finding competent people.
2. Too few or too many on the payroll.
3. They are not seeing enough patients.
4. They are keeping patients waiting too long.
5. They are not marketing to patients.
6. Patients are not treated in a manner that is sufficiently friendly.
7. There is frequent turnover of personnel.
8. The cost of staffing has reduced net.

OAWSDT

In our practice we used to call it OAWSDT: "Oh, Are We Still Doing That?" Last summer you and your staff agreed to clip newspaper items about prominent patients and hang them on the bulletin board. By mid-August you were doing it occasionally, and by November the yellowed paper was anything but current. Then, one day a patient looked over the material and commented, "You should have Sunday's feature on my cousin Fred hanging up there. He's a patient of yours." Sudden panic!

The scenario that follows could apply to almost anything: The doctor calls the staff together and demands, "Why aren't you watching the bulletin board?" (or suggesting spare contacts or new frames or almost anything else). The standard answer comes back, "OAWSDT."

At staff meetings in our office I used to close with an OAWSDT list pointing out the things that had slipped through the cracks of our daily routines.

Sustained activity counts. Emphasizing repetition, communication experts tell us never to try a "little" advertising, and the same applies to in-office promotion. We used to provide lunch for contact lens patients in our office for the long hours of observation required by early PMMA (Polymethyl Mecrylate) techniques. Now, 25 years later, patients still tell me how much they enjoyed that "extra" and many other bits of routine now long forgotten. A good idea usually has life long after we become bored. But, perhaps, boredom is the very reason people quit doing a thing.

"Oh, are we still doing that?" Remember when you used to keep fresh flowers in the office and give a rosebud to every lady who came in? How about the time you suggested that patients take home a magazine from the reception room if they hadn't finished reading an article or when you marked records for proper pronunciation of unusual patient names? A lot of OAWSDT can be prevented by performance reviews.

On the other hand, when OAWSDT creeps into a staff meeting, it may be time to take a serious look at the procedure and ask why? Perhaps it is a loser. Instead of letting them die a natural death, have the courage to scrap projects that aren't working. Tell your staff when it is time to quit.

Reviews

I show my employees how to shine, says optometrist Don Hoffer of Canoga Park, California. Writing in *Review of Optometry,* he says, "Experience has taught me that employees really want—and need—the kind of direction personal evaluation can give. Most are sincere in their desire to please you; you only need to tell them how" (Hoffer 1990). Evaluation begins with a private assessment of an employee's performance, a review which should never be made when you are tired or distracted. Your own mood shouldn't affect an employee's future. Then, follow a specific order of evaluation just as you would if you were examining a patient. He suggests a system used by the Bascom Palmer Eye Institute in Miami.

☐ ☐ ☐ ☐ ☐ **Employee Evaluation Checklist**

1. quality
2. quantity
3. knowledge of the job
4. dependability
5. attitude
6. initiative
7. appearance
8. absence of personal distractions
9. overall performance

This information alone will be worthless if it is not directed toward correcting errors and stimulating better performance. Share the ratings with your employees. Most will actually be excited about the review and anxious to hear your evaluation. Touch on each area and develop a plan for improvement as required. Most importantly, take the time to compliment employees on work well done.

For a quarter century, my staff could rely on a philosophy repeated during every job review: The right to make a decision includes the right to make a mistake!

When responsibility has been delegated, we employers have to accept the consequences. People will not do their best if they expect reprimand for honest errors in judgment.

Don't harp on poor choices. Those who make them usually know it and are hoping for a chance to correct the mistake. The courtesy and respect shown your office staff will be reflected when they deal with patients.

When All Else Fails

In a book that deals with marketing and promoting contact lens practice, the somewhat unrelated matter of dismissing employees may seem like extra baggage. I'm going to say a few words, though, because staff efficiency and morale are part of the game.

When someone isn't doing well, keep records of the unsatisfactory work involved, criticism, and warnings. Try to help the employee to reform, of course, by discussing specific problems and possible improvements, but if you must fire someone, don't wait.

Do it in your office, with the door closed. Make certain it's not a holiday or the person's birthday. Don't dwell on your affection for the individual nor stress your guilt or discomfort, just as you should not be too brisk or coldly businesslike. On the other extreme, don't hold out false hopes that the person will be hired again. This is as bad as allowing employees to stay on indefinitely.

Be thorough in describing your termination policy. Hopefully, you already know better than to discuss the reasons for firing someone with other members of the staff. If in doubt, this is also a fine time to consult your attorney. Above all, avoid "lame-duck" sessions. Nothing is more demoralizing than a "2-week notice" of dismissal.

Without doubt, the most difficult situation any employer faces is that of firing persons who work hard, doing the best they can, but whose self-confidence far outstrips ability. It is difficult to tell these people they are incompetent—after all, you may have given raises and promotions over the years and, to be blunt, it was you who put them in water over their heads. Furthermore, if the staff member has been there for any length of time, dismissal sends a clear message to the other employees. People stay only as long as they are useful and are dismissed without compassion after that. Help preserve the fired employee's dignity.

Even though it is tougher in a small office, the policy followed by most large corporations applies. In the matter of disciplinary policy it is a four-step procedure.

1. verbal reprimand (noted in writing in the employee's record)
2. written reprimand
3. written reprimand clearly indicating the third transgression
4. termination

Of course, verbal warning would not suffice for someone caught embezzling. Guidelines should be flexible enough to allow for appropriate handling of such matters.

Who will do the firing? If the executive assistant handles dismissals, it raises that employee's authority with the staff. But, on the down side, the executive's position as part of the employee "team" will suffer.

Continuing Education

Perhaps you have observed as I did many years ago the characteristic "UNs" of optometric assistants. On the average, they stay in the eye-care field only 5 years because they are

UNtrained
UNderpaid
UNappreciated
UNderutilized

Pay doesn't always come in the form of cash. Countless surveys have shown that recognition for a job well done is more important. So, it would seem that we can save money by showing appreciation for service, and, happily, that can come in the form of better education. In other words, take (or send) your staff to meetings.

You may say, "That would be OK if I had only one or two aides, but I have so many on my payroll I simply can't afford it." Nonsense. If your practice is large enough to justify such a staff, you certainly *can* afford it. The matter involves little more than budgeting as a percentage of salary. Just as you allocate health insurance, uniforms, F.I.C.A., etc., plan a specific allotment for Vision Expo, a regional meeting, or a state convention. The reward will be many times greater than the same dollar amount on a paycheck.

Get Your Staff Into the Act

Most of our employees are so wrapped up in the mechanics of running an office that they feel salesmanship involves little more than being nice to patients under trying circumstances. While we are trying to point out a relationship between attitude, practice volume, and take-home pay, we must at the same time avoid undermining the sense of security that goes with thinking the job has a future (Koetting 1990).

Set a good example? Sure, but couple it with a generous helping of whole-office participation and enthusiasm. Everyone loves something new. Advertising people tell us that "new" and "improved" are two of the strongest words one can use in printed copy. The same really applies to conversation: "Dr. Koetting has just come back from a conference with a whole lot of *new* information on fitting contacts for people with astigmatism." "We have just gotten our *new* autokeratometer (or computer, or bio, etc.), and we are like kids with a *new* toy. The doctor is in there waiting to show you how it works."

This is a fine time for them to be awe-struck: "This new instrument is *very* expensive." However, never, never state the actual price. Numbers mean different things to different people. Some may wonder how you can afford it, and others will compare it to some investment of their own. But, everyone will respect a "very expensive" commitment to better patient care. Be sure your assistants talk it up.

"Did you see the article about Dr. Koetting in last week's paper? We are all so proud of him." Or, "Congressman Smith's appointment has certainly received a lot of attention. You know, he's a patient in our offie." A few well-chosen positive comments will make a genuine lasting impression.

The best way to learn how to do something certainly does involve trying to teach it to someone else. Staff meetings can serve a dual purpose: simply have an assistant or technician who shows some marketing savvy demonstrate the technique to others in the office. It's contagious!

Everyone benefits from role playing. Someone acts the patient's part, while your assistant begins, "You know, Mrs. Jones, you could be taking better care of your eyes and saving money too, with a service agreement." Selling becomes a game once the ice is broken.

Sales Reps and Your Staff

How about a free consultant with someone who regularly visits 100 optometric practices, is willing to give you the time, knows a great deal about new products, and is experienced in marketing?

Ohio practice management expert Erwin Jay says you do just that when you talk to a laboratory representative. He points out that you may have to pay a consultant $3000 just to come into your office for a day, but a rep will consult with you for nothing.

You may have little time to train your staff, but most reps will provide educational sessions on topics from neutralizing glasses to using the telephone more effectively. Besides providing merchandising ads, like brochures and point-of-purchase displays, reps can often help you by showing your assistants how to use them.

Indiana practice management lecturer Neil Gailmard observes the role of reps as seeing that you get invited to prestigious seminars in exotic places. The same benefits can also be extended to technicians in your office.

Uniforms

There will be more to say on this subject when we talk about your image in the community, but here are a few observations based on 40 years' experience. Identifying your staff is just the beginning.

It Is Your Choice

Supplying career apparel is more than a fringe benefit. Doing so puts you in a position to suggest, or even demand, the style which is best suited to the practice. This choice includes more than color and design. Slacks, for example, are a more discreet choice for those who must frequently search out missing contacts, and your veto power on micro-minis is final as long as you pay the bills.

Consider, on the other hand, the embarrassment involved in telling an assistant that that person's clothing is dowdy or ready for the cleaners. "Sorry Boss, I just can't afford it, but I'm glad you brought up the matter because *I've* got a question for you." Sometimes telling an employee to spend money on clothing really isn't fair and is often a prelude to hard feelings.

Furthermore, well-made attractive uniforms boost morale, make a favorable impression on patients, and provide a genuine "status symbol" for an optometric aide. A uniform identifies the employee as a member of the health-care team and an important part of the doctor's practice.

Total Satisfaction Is Rare

In a small office, the assistant may wisely choose the uniform, but whenever three or more are involved, one person must be given the authority to select a style that will be universally attractive and assured the support to stay with that decision. After all, any purchase will wear out sooner or later, and suggestions or complaints can be considered again at that time.

Optometry's image has not always been clearly professional, so optometric personnel used to dress like nurses, medical technicians, and hospital orderlies. The need to identify with hospital white (which is usually green or blue nowadays anyway) is no longer pressing. Colorful contemporary clothing adds a touch of class.

We found that styles become obsolete and uniforms begin to look shabby after about 50 wearings. Thus, a full-time employee with three changes will be ready for a complete replacement every 6 months. Some people seem to wear clothing out more rapidly than others, but in the interest of conformity, uniforms are best purchased in the spring and fall. Without limitations, this provides the added advantage of seasonally appropriate clothing.

Offices become chilly when the air conditioner overreacts or during unexpected changes in the weather. Some sort of jacket or blazer ought to be included and integrated with the basic style. That lovely sweater Aunt Elsa knitted last Christmas simply destroys the whole effect—no exceptions.

And then there's jewelry. A name tag and a registered assistant's pin belong in plain sight. All other pins, necklaces, pendants, and the like are as taboo as mesh hose and sandals.

Shoes are included and should be supplied twice a year. Coordinated in color, they should be selected for comfort and quality rather than fashion. Choosing shoes by major manufacturers will ensure a good fit for everyone and continuing supply as needed.

Like it or not, staff changes occur; so, when buying ready-made outfits, get assurance from the supplier that the style will be in stock *in all sizes* for at least 6 months. If the uniforms are custom made, the same holds true where the material is concerned. Either way, delivery time is important and a firm understanding will prevent disappointment and confusion later. And don't forget to mention that clothing allowances are an employee benefit.

Your Employee Manual

At the risk of seeming cavalier on the subject, I'm going to say that you should have an employee manual or "office bible" and let it go at that. There seems little need to repeat advice that has been published in so many places by so many people. Just remember that you need a list of rules and regulations.

Temporary Employees

In a field as specialized as ours, finding technical help on a temporary basis is almost impossible, except for recruiting retirees and those who have turned to homemaking as a career.

Secretarial help is another matter. What happens when your "right arm" is home with the flu? A competent temporary employee can ease the tension by handling a good chunk of the clerical work. Temps, nowadays, can do much more.

About a million temporary employees work each week in jobs ranging from secretary to CEO, according to the National Association of Temporary Services. One out of every hundred people working in the nonagricultural segment of our economy during a typical work week is on a temporary payroll. You may be willing to take advantage of the service, but don't wait until the last minute. A few basic guidelines can lead you to the right agency when you need one.

Assess an agency's recruiting, testing, and evaluation procedures by asking what kinds of tests have been administered to employees. Otherwise, you may discover too late that a self-professed word processor doesn't know a keyboard from a floppy disk. Try to work with an agency that has in-house training facilities, and ask how the temp's performance has been monitored.

Any reliable service will make an arrival check about 15 minutes after the temporary was scheduled to start the workday, making sure the person showed up on time and that you are satisfied. A similar check should be made in mid-afternoon of the first day to be certain the work is satisfactory. And, try to pick an established firm. The longer an agency has been in existence, the more experience its owner has and the more likely they will be to select temporary help that will fit your needs.

8

□ □ □
□ □ □
□ □ □

Communication

The information was presented in a most unusual place, and that adds to its credibility: At the 1989 meeting of the American Academy of Optometry, Briony Thompson and a team of Australians reported study results showing that contact lens wearers' motivation, satisfaction, and compliance were significantly associated with their clinician's interpersonal skills (Collins, Thompson, and Hearn 1989). Everything from appointment-keeping to lens care and satisfaction with contact lens fit related to empathy, information exchange, willingness to explain, clarity of instructions, and the optometrist's comfort in the interaction. Clinicians, they concluded, should learn skills for patient management in addition to clinical examination techniques.

A Harris poll reported that people get 78.4% of their information on contact lenses from friends, relatives, and neighbors—our patients. Obviously, they must be reminded how well we have cared for them in the past and how important it is for them to seek continuing care. A 1-hour visit with the optometrist is all too quickly forgotten.

Well, how can you improve patient communication skills? Start by getting the facts. Call it case history if you will, but there is much more to it. Find out what your patients want to say.

1. *Start with the telephone.* The standard "How may I help you?" is really where it all begins. Why does anyone call your office? Do you *really* understand the purpose of the visit? Be sure your receptionist is asking, "How are your eyes troubling you?"
2. *The patient information form.* "Welcome to Our Office" is a pretty standard heading for a variety of forms designed to collect address and billing information. Most wind up with the who-referred-you-to-us question. Read it and look up the referring party's record. You have a mutual friend!
3. *Background history.* Include personal information and comments in the case history. (Not just "student," but what school, and is there a relationship with other patients who go there? Who else works for the company, etc.?)

4. *Pre-exam questionnaires.* Detailed history is usually included in the pre-examination questionnaires used in many offices. Pick out minutiae to prove you are paying attention.
5. *Establish rapport.* Make conversation on impersonal matters, like the weather if all else fails. Current news is a whole lot better if you are staying on top of things and the topic isn't too controversial.
6. *Listen.* Listening is the key to understanding and influencing other people.

In *Thriving On Chaos*, Tom Peters put it succinctly (Peters 1987): Listening means paying attention.

□ □ □ □ □ How To Be a Good Listener

- Don't interrupt.
- Try to find the main idea.
- Fight distractions.
- Don't become emotional.
- Take notes if you can.
- Let others talk first.
- Follow up with questions.

The High-Tech Approach

An innovative method introduced in 1990 may change the way a lot of us will take case histories in the future. The NICHE 1 INSIGHT™ (Ceresco Marketing, Inc.) electronic interview uses a touch-sensitive screen that enables patients to describe lifestyles and needs without filling out a form. Based on the patient's prior responses, follow-up queries that target the issues each patient considers important are asked.

The computer then selects successive questions and predicts hundreds of possible discrete answers to complete the patient's profile. A printed report summarizes each patient's unique needs, attitudes, values, and expectations in detail along with emotional motivators that control buying decisions.

Things People Remember

Looking back, we're often embarrassed at ourselves. Why in the world do we care about and remember trivial, ridiculous things that should have been forgotten?

Why? Because it's not only difficult but almost impossible to erase slights from memory. The smallest one by the most inconsequential person is stored somewhere, waiting to surface again at some unrelated moment. How long ago was it that someone said you looked like a theater usher in your expensive new blazer? And why, when the blazer has long since gone to a thrift shop, does the remark still float back into your mind?

A brushoff during a cocktail party should mean as little as such parties themselves do. So what if someone being introduced to you mutters a perfunctory "How do you do" and turns away to talk to someone else? Your mind says "forget it," but there is an emotion to deal with. So it is with patients who feel they should get full attention in your office.

□ □ □ □ □ **How to Handle Complaints**

Countless studies and reports have shown that an unhappy patient who has a problem resolved is very likely to return. The process of hearing and acting upon a complaint will be remembered quite favorably, enough so that the original cause may be overlooked or even forgiven. But, suppose that patient is *downright mad*. In emotional situations, feelings take priority over facts. Here are some things you can do:

1. Start the conversation from a comfortable distance and initiate eye contact.
2. Show concern in everything you do.
3. Take notes if necessary and repeat the story to be sure you have the facts straight.
4. Give the upset patient your undivided active attention.
5. Ask how the patient feels about the situation.
6. Make a special note of remedies that have already been tried.
7. Acknowledge anything that is valid by saying things like "you are absolutely correct, etc."
8. Never admit it is a common problem, and try to avoid saying it has previously occurred.
9. If you cannot agree, try to show that the policy is fair and that a different approach would lead to greater problems.
10. Admit the error if one was made.
11. Accept the complaint as if you welcomed the advice and do not show resentment.
12. Communicate that you want to keep this person as a patient.

□ □ □ □ □ The Five Worst Phrases to Say on the Telephone

Nancy Friedman calls herself "The Telephone Doctor" and conducts seminars in St. Louis. Carrying on what she calls a neverending battle against rudeness, unfriendliness, and lousy customer service, she encourages banning the following five phrases from every employee's telephone conversation.

1. "I don't know." There is no real need for these three words. Outside of sensitive financial data, there is really no information that shouldn't be available. Instead, say, "That's a good question. Let me check and find out." Then go *find out.*

2. "We can't do that." This one is guaranteed to get the patient's blood boiling. Far better to reply, "That's a tough one. Let's see what we can do about it," while looking for alternative solutions. If none exist, ask for a suggestion from the patient. Often times, the second request will be much easier to handle.

3. "You'll have to." Wrong! The only thing callers have to do is die and pay taxes. With that line you may rest assured they won't. Use phrases such as "Here's how we can help you with that," or "The next time that happens, here's what you can do." (Almost as bad is "What was your name?" as though the caller is no longer with us.)

4. "Hang on a second I'll be right back." Try telling the truth. "It may take me 2 or 3 minutes to get the information. Are you able to hold while I check?" Be ready to call back.

5. "No" at the beginning of a sentence. The word *no* is useless and conveys total rejection. Most sentences are grammatically correct without it. If you think before you speak, you can turn every answer into a positive response.

□ □ □ □ □ Office Acoustics

Except for my private office and the conference room, I practiced for 40 years without closing a door. Other than conversation, what goes on in an optometric office that would require so much privacy? OK, you agree, but isn't conversation the very reason doors are needed? Not if the place is designed right. Furthermore, new patients—especially those of the opposite gender—feel a lot better if the exit isn't blocked. Here are some of the things we've incorporated to keep communication private with the doors open:

1. carpets
2. acoustical ceilings
3. wall carpet for practical decorating elegance
4. standard doorways, no large openings
5. background music
6. speakers in the halls and public areas, but never in examining rooms
7. no partitions that do not reach the ceiling
8. a floor plan that prevents patients from facing into other rooms
9. bookshelves and vertical files
10. solid construction

The Written Word

Communicating with patients not only involves expressing yourself clearly but tailoring your message to the needs, concerns, temperament, and even the vocabulary of your audience. One-on-one communication calls for somewhat different strategies and skills than a presentation or a speech, although if you start by focusing on the individual, the rest of the message will come quite naturally as required.

When you prepare any document—a brochure, correspondence, or a newsletter—start with a specific goal. There are four basics of document preparation, and it won't hurt to keep them in mind no matter how trivial the message may seem.

□ □ □ □ □ The Four Basics of Document Preparation

1. *Aim for a specific result.* Include short- or long-range objectives if necessary, and be sure you know exactly what you want the patient to comprehend.
2. *Always take a positive approach.* Be sure your words communicate your personal enthusiasm to the patient.
3. *Don't forget the senses.* Include some tailored images that are light and friendly (i.e., "Your note was like a breath of spring," or "We all cheered when your lenses arrived").
4. *Match your desires to the patient's needs.* Benefits, benefits, benefits! Always imagine the reader asking, "What's in it for me?"

Logos

Everything printed in your office should tie together, and some graphic design will help people keep you in mind. You will probably need special help with this, and as you work with the artist, remember these four basic components:

1. *Color.* Strong colors grab attention and particularly appeal to younger people. Pastels elicit feelings of restfulness and tenderness. Raised embossing or metallic gold and silver indicate elegance and richness. A gold-stamped logo on your letterhead can be used to carry the theme to other places, such as lens cases, name tags, or even special gifts for patients.

2. *Typestyle.* Typestyles have different personalities. Levi Strauss uses a strong square typestyle that looks as tough as its pants, but O.D.s will do better with something more professional.

3. *Content.* Logo content is often symbolic. Prudential has a rock; Apple computers show the fruit with a missing bite (byte). If you want to stress service, use lines that imply speed.

4. *Size.* A too-large bold logo may deprive you of the professional distinction that is better suited to your practice.

Be Sure Your Letters Are Read

Individual correspondence is one thing; form letters are something else. According to direct-mail marketers, readers look first at the salutation of a letter. In a nonpersonalized letter, they focus on the headline. Then they glance at the signature. Next they read the P.S. Only then do they go back and maybe start to read the letter. This certainly suggests adding a postscript—it may be the most important part. Some of the most effective letters and memos I've received have also made good use of color.

□ □ □ □ □ **How to Personalize Your Letters**

- Add a handwritten note, preferably in brightly colored ink.
- Circle key words in color (use a highlighter), or put some vertical marks in the margin.
- When the letter is a form going to many people, write the name in color, by hand, in the top margin.
- Call special attention by adding an adhesive-backed note with some personal message.
- Use a wordprocessor to make each form letter look personal.

Newsletters

This is certainly not a new idea, and as a matter of fact, I have rarely used them. Maybe I just wanted to be different and felt that as long patients received *something* on a regular schedule, it was just as effective and the variety would attract some attention. Newsletters are nevertheless a versatile communication tool that many consider an economical, well-received professional marketing device. They should be written to

- accurately represent you and your staff
- convey information that is useful and interesting
- make the reader feel a part of the conversation and never that you are talking down

Obviously, by creating your own newsletters, you can make them as personal and specific as you wish. Don't be afraid to collect samples from other professionals. There are plenty of publishers who are looking for your business. Hire one if you wish, or use their representative work as a guideline while considering what your patients want to know and the types of questions they are likely to ask.

Keep your newsletter short if you want it read, but additional advice should come from a layout artist or printer. Select these folks according to your budget, and get some recommendations from professionals or business people in your community.

□ □ □ □ □ Steps in Preparing a Newsletter

1. *Layout.* Show the printer a sample, or get some help from an artist.
2. *Copy.* Proofread it carefully for spelling, grammar, and punctuation.
3. *Proof.* Check the printer's proof again for errors. If headline placement and photos don't please you, say so.
4. *Paper.* Select a stock that is heavy enough so the print will not show through, with a color and texture that makes photos look good, but light enough to use with an accompanying cover letter while keeping the total weight under the 1-ounce postage limit.
5. *Color.* Use two. It doesn't cost that much more.

Brochures

A first-rate practice brochure is essential. We've touched on this subject in previous chapters. If you don't have one now, get one.

☐ ☐ ☐ ☐ ☐ Five Reasons to use a Brochure

1. as a powerful first impression for new patients
2. to reinforce ties with existing patients
3. to create a sense of identity for your staff and boost morale
4. as a direct-mail piece
5. to confirm appointments and eliminate misunderstanding by confirming office policies in print

☐ ☐ ☐ ☐ ☐ Printing Brochures Effectively

The cover must have a catchy, benefit-oriented headline supported by attractive graphics that will lure readers into its content (Figure 8.1). Most authorities suggest that professionals include a brief biography. *Brochures should*

1. be printed on both sides and folded to fit in a #10 envelope
2. coordinate with your office stationery and other printed materials
3. use two ink colors and colored paper stock
4. vary typestyles and use upper- and lowercase letters to make reading easier
5. be clearly printed with large type and plenty of white space
6. spell out all conditions of patient care that will be important to the reader
7. use your name several times in obvious locations

☐ ☐ ☐ ☐ ☐ How to Write Effective Copy

The best brochures are often those with the least copy, usually one to three paragraphs on each topic (Figure 8.2). Try not to think of filling space, but ask yourself how to prepare the shortest possible message that will get your point across.

1. Use personal pronouns (you, we, my, I, and our).
2. Avoid describing policies as though they were etched in stone.
3. Use short headlines, and write them after the copy is complete.
4. Keep paragraphs to one topic and a manageable length, usually no more than nine or ten lines.
5. Avoid sexist language by substituting "you" for "he," "him," and "his."
6. Aim for consistency of tone so that all sections sound as if they were written by the same person.

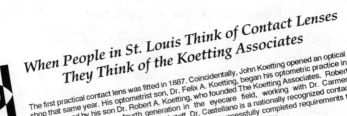

When People in St. Louis Think of Contact Lenses They Think of the Koetting Associates

The first practical contact lens was fitted in 1887. Coincidentally, John Koetting opened an optical shop that same year. His optometrist son, Dr. Felix A. Koetting, began his optometric practice in 1921, followed by his son Dr. Robert A. Koetting, who founded The Koetting Associates. Robert R. Koetting, represents a fourth generation in the eyecare field, working with Dr. Carmen Castellano, as he heads the professional staff. Dr. Castellano is a nationally recognized contact lens specialist and is one of only 200 persons to have successfully completed requirements to become a Diplomate of the prestigious American Academy of Optometry.

~loning what has often been called the country's best run contact lens practice, The Koetting
~hered to a strict philosophy of personnel training and continuing education
~hing, as evidenced by the fact that 92% of the more than 20,000
~t lens experience before coming to their office. Addition-
~om wears contact lenses to better understand
~os has shown that poor handling
~perienced instructors are

Which Lens is Best?

Don't worry! After reviewing all of the factors, your doctor will suggest the one that's right for you. The staff at The Koetting Associates work with every brand of lens and plastic. The following general descriptions will help you understand the differences between lens types but keep in mind that the way a lens fits is more important than the material from which it's made.

RIGID lenses were called "hard contacts" for many years. When newer oxygen transmitting plastics were developed, promoters started calling them rigid gas permeable (RGP) or "semi-soft". There is a significant difference between the old and new plastics, but the way a lens fits really determines how it feels.

SOFT contacts are flexible. They are sometimes known as hydrophilic lenses because they actually attract and absorb moisture. Soft lenses are made from material that conforms to the shape of the eye so perfectly that most people who try them on for the first time cannot believe they are actually wearing contacts. In recent years the daily hygienic care for these lenses has become significantly easier requiring less time and fewer care products.

COMBINATION hard and soft lenses are constructed with a rigid center surrounded by a soft "skirt". They include the best and possibly the worst features of both types. Your doctor will prescribe them if they will be helpful in your case.

Figure 8.1 Welcome to your patients. A practical informative brochure is important. Patients want and need to know something of the doctor's background and frequently have questions that are never asked. Put it in print.

7. Use contractions as you would in speaking.
8. Write in the *active* rather than *passive* voice (say "we believe" instead of "it is our belief that").

Figure 8.2 Get personal. Patients are glad to know that the doctor is human too. Speak directly, and say what you mean.

9. Avoid content that may become dated, such as staff names or "last year during the earthquake."

10. Put statements in positive form. For example, say "We are almost always on schedule" instead of "We do not very often fall behind schedule."
11. Omit needless words. Almost all copy contains "that" and "the" in a dozen unnecessary places.
12. Use conventional spelling, and avoid unusual words.
13. Revise and rewrite. Even professionals rarely send their first attempts to the printer.

Direct Mail

Simply defined, direct mail is unsolicited advertising or promotional material (that is, material the recipient has not requested) delivered to an individual or company by the Postal Service (Figures 8.3 and 8.4). Marketing that way, however, is anything but simple. It is big business. For proof, just look in your mailbox.

According to the Direct Marketing Association (DMA), third-class mail amounts to 63 billion pieces and accounts for almost one-third of all advertising expenditures, substantially exceeding television.

Chet Dalzell of the DMA encourages professionals to pursue narrow market niches wherever possible. The more you can identify the specific needs of your target market, the better you can address them.

□ □ □ □ □ Advantages of Using Direct Mail

Chet Gnam, a direct-mail specialist, lists these advantages of using direct-mail pieces:

1. *Measurement.* You can achieve greater measured results.
2. *Flexibility.* You can be as expansive as you wish, or your mailings can be tailored to concise interests.
3. *Selectivity.* You can zero in on almost any target audience and eliminate costly exposure to disinterested groups.
4. *Personalization.* Use your name in any number of ways.
5. *Response.* Direct mail achieves the highest percentage of response per thousand people reached.
6. *Testing.* You have an unlimited opportunity to test any part of your program on a specific audience.
7. *Extensive reach.* You may think your practice is too small to compete with the giants, but with direct mail you can compete with anyone.

Figure 8.3 Patient ID card. How to you get attention when you mail something to a patient? Be different! Newsletters and informative brochures are fine, but anything personalized gets more attention.

Lists

There are basically two kinds of mailing lists: your own patient records and everything else. Recall notices, newsletters, and the like go to people who have already been to your office. That's easy; how about the others?

If you wish to send information to a specific group, there is almost certainly a local organization to which these people belong (for example, the mailing list of an older-adult group, country club membership rosters, and the like). Other lists can be rented from firms that maintain extensive computer information on people by age, sex, occupation, special interest, and location. Zip

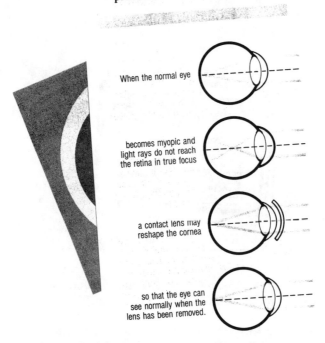

What about Orthokeratology?

Or·tho·kera·tol´ogy

Orthokeratology: the reduction, modification or elimination of refractive anomalies by the programmed application of contact lenses or other related procedures.

When the normal eye

becomes myopic and light rays do not reach the retina in true focus

a contact lens may reshape the cornea

so that the eye can see normally when the lens has been removed.

Figure 8.4 A short informative pamphlet. Mailing pamphlets on various subjects awakens patients to the variety of services performed in your office. Because there is a wide variety of printed material available, this is probably the least expensive way of keeping in touch.

code lists by "occupant" are much cheaper (and they should be). Mailing-list firms can generally give you what you want and will charge for each usage.

Selecting a Mailer

The first step in choosing a direct-mail firm is to know what you are looking for. Direct mail is geared to those who seek a measurable response. Look for a company that talks about the costs versus return in terms of dollars. You should expect to know how much your return will be and how much it will cost.

Many firms provide traditional advertising and promotional expertise, including writing and graphic design. Others provide only lists, while some combine all or part of these services. You probably won't find one, but look for those with experience in the eye-care field.

Before you execute a full-blown program, try different offers and different approaches on a small sample of names. A typical one-time mailing list rental is $50 to $90 per 1000 names, including the broker's fee. You can't photocopy lists legally, but you can add to your files anyone who responds to your mailing.

Timing counts in direct mail. January, February, and September are traditionally good marketing months. The summer is poor. If you use first-class mail, time it so your mailer doesn't arrive on a Monday or just after a holiday. The 15th and 30th of the month—paydays—are said to be good choices. You can save money by mailing third-class bulk rate if you have at least 200 identical pieces bundled according to zip code. Your post office can provide details.

Instruction and Compliance

Patients don't always follow wearing instructions, sometimes out of ignorance, although a number are downright recalcitrant. A good number of contact lens wearers are apt to make honest mistakes. Long before compliance became a serious issue, optometric practice management pioneer George Elmstrom advised

1. oral instruction and demonstration
2. film or video
3. literature
4. follow-up

There are some things to be said about tapes, i.e., video and audio cassettes. Although using tapes to provide information and instructions is standard procedure now, we've been using this method for a long time. The addition of a VCR to your reception area provides a continuing opportunity to educate a captive audience. The AOA has tapes available on topics ranging from children's vision to safe driving. And, of course, on contact lenses. Moreover, every lens and solution manufacturer has produced something at one time or another. Don't worry about making your own; they're out there for the asking.

On the other hand, our office never used material prepared by someone else. We take the video very seriously and keep two programs running most of the time. A general description of the office and exam procedure is shown in the reception room. This video covers some background history of the practice and includes safety tips on contact lens wear, so it will be of interest to new and repeat patients. It is about 15 minutes long.

The other tapes run about 10 minutes and are designed for rigid or soft lens wearers. These are shown in the contact lens instruction rooms.

The video components of color, light, and sound, together with a succinct script, are hundreds of times more effective than a spoken presentation. But, such visual aids can't take the place of teaching and probably won't save an instructor's time. They simply ensure that patients receive complete information in an unhurried manner. This in turn fulfills much of the legal responsibility.

Now Hear This

Unlike videotapes, audio cassettes are inexpensive and convenient. We provide each of our contact lens patients with easy-to-understand instructions on tape. Because they are duplicated in quantity, they cost only about $2 per patient. To listen, new lens wearers need only an audio-cassette player that can be used in the bathroom or wherever they care for lenses. In addition to obvious patient compliance benefits, tapes have a genuine PR value. Family, friends, and neighbors will listen or even borrow them for personal use. And preparing one takes less work than you might think.

□ □ □ □ □ How to Make an Audio Instruction Tape

1. *Script.* You will probably need four. One for application and another for removal of RGP lenses, plus two more for hydrogels. Try to keep the length of each about 5 or 6 minutes, matching them so both sides of the tape will be the same length.
2. *Take it easy.* Make sure what you say sounds natural and conversational. You might even consider using a recorder to tape yourself giving "live" instructions to a patient.
3. *A master tape.* Your original tape will probably need to be edited, so it's best to use a radio station or professional studio. An amateur technician is less expensive, but the results may not be as good. (This will probably cost between $50 and $500.)
4. *The voice.* Decide who will be speaking. You can do it yourself, but professional announcers are easy to find. Just call a local radio station and ask if anyone would like a free-lance job. (This will cost about $100.) An ad agency or PR firm could handle the whole process for you, but it will be expensive and the tape may not say what you really want. You might also include some background music for which there will probably be an additional charge.
5. *Duplicates.* Once you have the master cassettes, multiple copies

are produced by a tape-duplicating service. Get recommendations from your previous contacts or check the Yellow Pages. Expect to pay about $1 per tape, including labels and boxes.

The cost per unit will evidently depend upon the total, but you should be able to keep it under $2 even if you make fewer than 1000.

Public Information

Put on a seminar. Lots of people do it. Run an ad, send out a mailing, give releases to the local media. Put on a show!

More and more professionals in the health-care field are presenting public information seminars. They rent a hall, hotel room, or even hold them in their own offices. Everybody has eyes, and people want to know about their vision. New techniques, especially in contact lenses, are attractive. Bring in an outside "expert," or do the job yourself. In any event, you'll want to do it right.

Frederick Gilbert says the tone of a technical presentation is by nature impersonal and objective. Because the content is often dry, the tricky part is presenting objective information to subjective human beings. The first rule involves making the content easy to understand. When a technical talk becomes information-dense, says Gilbert, listeners get overwhelmed and simply tune out.

☐ ☐ ☐ ☐ ☐ Characteristics of a Good Speaker

- Content is important, but it isn't everything. Use a friendly speaking style.
- It's not OK to "data dump" on technical people just because they are bright.
- The speaker is more important than the projector.
- Enthusiasm counts. Boring presentations are frustrating and regarded as a waste of time.
- Technical talks should be more than informational, they should be persuasive.
- Don't use too many visuals. Less is more.
- Use color graphs and charts rather than word slides, and keep visuals big and bold.
- Deliver your talk with enough style and audience involvement to keep people interested.

One of my college instructors pointed out that, except for some rare moments of introspection, all speaking is public speaking. The size of the audience may vary from one to many thousands, but the communication skills involved are no more or less important.

9

□ □ □
□ □ □
□ □ □

Your Image in the Community

Who Are You?

Does more success come to those who look successful? You bet it does! And, while you're about it, don't underestimate the "doctor" image.

Even though Frankenstein was a loser, Kildare was a saint. Marcus Welby, warm, unhurried, and always right, picked up his TV generation, followed in turn by the cast of "M*A*S*H," bearing their anguish in pranks and alcohol. The doctors of "St. Elsewhere" were more human, but despite their disordered lives, won public respect as they helped save *most* of their patients.

Like it or not, eye care is a part of this public conception. It is ours to use or abuse and a potentially powerful practice-building tool. Dentists have consistently been portrayed as heartless sadists, while nurses may be docile handmaidens to male doctors, severe and cruel like Ms. Ratched in *One Flew Over the Cuckoo's Nest,* or even sexpots like Hot-Lips Houlihan. Fortunately, it may not be too late to hitch a ride on the Welby-Kildare image.

Of course, degrees and titles as such don't mean what they used to. Big corporations, such as IBM or General Dynamics, hire Ph.D.s like Greyhound hires bus drivers. And, titles are somewhat ambiguous: Doc Severinsen, Colonel Sanders, or Captain Kangaroo. So, there is more to it than a traditional designation. What *we* think we are determines what other people perceive us to be.

Your lifestyle, your position in the community, and achievement of your goals will depend on what you think a doctor should be, should say, should do, and how a doctor should think and act. There is still plenty of room for old-fashioned "elegance."

Who Do You Think You Are?

We're talking about spats and a walking stick (although there may be a place for them, too), and I'm certainly not talking about snobbery.

The person with true "class" is not a snob. He or she isn't trying to win; that person has already won and knows it.

A few years ago my office was within easy walking distance of my home, so I occasionally commuted on foot. Once, I was walking to work feeling kind of low about something, and I decided to perk up. I squared my shoulders, put my head back, and began to take long straight strides forward. I just wanted to look and feel as though I owned the world, and it worked.

As I marched along the sidewalk, an involuntary smile crossed my face, and I was almost oblivious of the world, until an automobile pulled up and the driver rolled down his window. "Hey," he said, "You must be a politician." You are what you think you are, and what you think you are will be understood and respected.

A "doctor" can have class without being a snob. I once found myself in emergency care at a local hospital following one of my several heart attacks. Checking in about 10:00 P.M., my body was immediately attached to the usual array of tubes and monitors and given sedation. About 11 o'clock, a young man awakened me and insisted on taking a lengthy case history, followed by a painful repositioning of the tubes and wires, while my legs dangled over the edge of the bed so he could check my reflexes by tapping my knees.

About midnight, I was awakened by another young man who did the exact same thing, asking the exact same questions, and checking my reflexes once more. I fell asleep, only to be reawakened about 1:30 A.M. by a third person repeating the very same questions.

This time I rebelled. "I know this is a teaching hospital," I said, "I know you must learn, but this is ridiculous. Please read my chart!"

The answer was classic: "*They* were learning," he sneered aloofly, "*I* am the *resident*." Your image in the community should not be that of a person who keeps his or her nose in the air like the *resident* (but at least he was self-assured). In his early books, Bob Levoy continually warned against the ITA: the Ivory Tower Attitude.

The ALPs in Your Neighborhood

I will admit picking these words to fit the acronym. ALP, and a good many other terms might fit, as well. But, no matter how you phrase it, your community image stands on three legs and it will topple if one part is missing. Think of them as the ALPs.

Achievement
Leadership
Profile

Achievers

Being an achiever in your community involves some things that may seem pretty obvious, but they warrant a closer look. You might start by picking a role model. The idea is certainly not as frivolous as it might sound at first (Johnson 1987).

Pick a successful competitor if you like, but you may do better taking a good hard look at the movers and shakers in any other field. Don't worry about the end result; you probably won't head a billion dollar company or build a highway. Look at *how* these people do things. I used to watch the late mayor of St. Louis, for whom the gigantic new convention center is named, working his way through a crowd. "Hi, I'm Al Cervantes," he would say to everyone, taking no chances on a lack of identification—an achiever with a very high profile. You know some of them, too. Study them.

Be a Leader

Americans need leaders, says Burt Nanus in his book *The Leader's Edge* (Nanus 1989). He thinks that leaders are self-trained and offers quite a list of suggestions. Here are some of them:

□ □ □ □ □ **How to Become a Leader**

- Know your goals.
- Seek responsibilities early and often.
- Develop far sightedness; look toward the future.
- Master the skills of interdependence. They are more important than meeting the competition.
- Develop personal character, integrity, and trust.
- Think like a researcher; develop a sense of curiosity and creativity. Be a problem-solver.
- Enjoy what you do.

Warren Bennis, in his best-seller, *On Becoming a Leader*, says that the mythical look of a leader is precisely that: a myth (Bennis 1989). Leaders come in all sizes, shapes, and dispositions. What they share in common, however, are several basic ingredients.

Effective leaders, he says, have a clear idea of what they want to do in both their professional and personal lives. They also possess the strength to pursue this vision despite the inevitable setbacks and failures. Leaders love what they do, love to do it, and communicate this feeling in ways that inspire others.

Leaders understand what they want to do and why and, more importantly, never lie to themselves or anyone else. They develop maturity by following rather than giving orders and earn their status through dedication and observation.

The fact that people trust a leader is more a product of leadership than an ingredient of it. It is the one quality that cannot be acquired. It can only be earned.

Bennis tells us that true leaders want to learn as much as they can, and they are willing to take risks, experiment, and innovate in the process. They wring knowledge and wisdom from every mistake and learn from adversity.

Create a High Profile

A few years ago, Dr. Joyce Brothers wrote *How to Get Whatever You Want Out of Life,* which included her 25 rules for succeeding in business (Brothers 1978). Rule #20, "Make Yourself Visible," simply states: "You will never be promoted, never considered for executive status, never made head of a management committee if no one knows you are there. Make sure people know who you are and what you do." One good road to visibility, she continues, is volunteering for civic activities or becoming active in professional societies.

Dick Sowby, O.D., of Burbank, California, suggests tying into some event, like "Save Your Vision Week," by inviting the mayor or another prominent person in your community to come in for a free examination and publicity photo. An eclipse is always a great time to make statements on safe viewing procedures, he adds.

One Way to Do It

Where to begin? Few things command more respect than the printed word. Publish or perish; but, what if you can't write? Or, even if you can, where will you find the time and how will that help anyway?

Having been active in the National Speakers Association for a good many years, I've listened to a lot of advice—pros talking to pros. If there has been a common denominator among these people who are so dedicated to self-promotion, it must be the need to see one's name in print. One well-known speaker openly shared the information that he has more than 160 finished articles filed and waiting for anyone to ask. Getting one's name in newsprint is important, of course, but being an author implies a much higher level of credibility.

So you aren't sure you can write? Not to worry, there are plenty of people out there who write for a living.

More than 40,000 new books are published each year in the United States alone. Most people outside of the publishing world assume that all of these books are the results of the lonely efforts of scribes whose interesting ideas are matched with their noteworthy writing talent. I wrote this myself (in case you're wondering), but by knowing how and where to get help, you can see your own ideas in a book, journal paper, or article.

Ghostwriters are a very expensive option, but one requiring minimal commitment from you. Most ghostwriters, working with your concept for a book, will interview you on tape, do additional research on their own, and submit a draft for your approval. Then, based on your feedback, they will edit the material into a finished manuscript. Expect to pay $25 to $100 an hour for an experienced writer. That's over $10,000 per book, so alternative ways to spend your promotional budget might be more appealing.

Collaborating with another author may avoid the somewhat unsavory reputation of ghostwriting. The American Society of Journalists and Authors (1501 Broadway, New York, New York 10036) even provides a "dial-a-writer" service at 212 997-0947. Local chapters of the National Writers Union can refer you to experienced persons, and, of course, you could advertise in writer's magazines or a large local newspaper.

Another approach involves hiring a consultant, who, for a fixed fee, will read your typed manuscript, frankly assess its strengths and weaknesses, and provide detailed suggestions for improvement and a list of publishers. They advertise under "Consultants-Publishing," but be wary lest you stumble into the clutches of a "vanity" or subsidy publisher who specializes in exploiting hopeful, naive authors.

Speak Up

Although public speaking consumes a great deal of personal time, for the amount of effort involved, I have observed that a short talk before a group of local citizens will generally yield a surprising number of new patients. Still, most of us would rather do just about anything else.

PTA and parents club members want to know about vision. Even the most fundamental facts are important to them and require very little research or preparation. Businesspeople and the Rotary or Chamber of Commerce are interested in industry needs, and ladies' clubs may want to hear more about tinted contacts. Many subjects we take for granted are genuinely interesting to a lot of people. Another sure-fire way to get booked takes no more effort than volunteering for the United Way, your local art museum, or a school bond campaign. Every cause has a speakers bureau.

Unfortunately, even seasoned orators feel a tinge of fear now and then. People experience "stage fright" to different degrees, and practice is the answer. Help is no further away than your local Dale Carnegie chapter or an adult education course. Joining a Toastmasters Club is even easier. Contrary to public misconceptions, this is not an organization of polished speakers (some members are probably the world's worst), so you will have the opportunity to talk before a sympathetic audience (Brooks 1966; Osgood 1989).

Because you will know your subjects, using cue cards, or no props at all, will help you look your best. Remember, without special training, it is very difficult, if not impossible, to write material that sounds like talk. Very few people can read effectively, even when a speech is well written, so you should stay with a speaking vocabulary. Regardless of the topic, the whole idea is to use words that sound conversational and to keep the choice at a level the audience will understand. If you must read something, go over every word aloud to be sure that you understand and believe what you are going to say.

The primary purpose of rehearsing is to become familiar enough with your presentation so that you can look up at your audience at least half of the time, and that takes plenty of practice. As you rehearse, you will also find places that need minor revisions or additional emphasis.

- Deliver your talk aloud and while standing.
- Practice with a warm body in the room (spouse, child, etc.).
- A tape recording may come as a shock, but it can be quite helpful.

Public speaking doesn't come easily for most of us. The opportunities are limited, and there will be many temptations to find some other approach to community recognition. These facts notwithstanding, those of us who have tried report no regrets and we have even learned to enjoy the applause. Pick up the telephone and call the president (if you don't know the program chairman) of the Kiwanis Club and say, "There are a lot of new things happening in my field that would probably interest your members." That's all there is to it.

□ □ □ □ □ Rules of Public Speaking

- Start with a slight pause, look at the audience, and smile.
- Be sure to speak slowly, low, clearly, and with some expression.
- Talk only about things you know.
- Look at the audience, and be conversational. Know when to stop. If you quit too soon, and the audience is interested, there will be questions. If not, they will be grateful.

What's in a Name?

Keeping a high profile means just that. People must know *you* are there—meaning, among other things, use the name your mother gave you! Not since the great immigrations of the nineteenth century, it seems, have people been so anxious to be called something else—"cute names on frame boutiques (Private Eyes), small practices trying to look big (Optometric Associates), and those who aspire to be official providers for the community (The Greater New York Contact Lens Clinic). In a large city, even those of us in the field need a score card to know who is in which practice. My own local telephone directory, for example, lists the following:

Eye Associates, Ltd.	Eye Institute
Eye Associates of South County	Eye Microsurgery
Eyecare Associates, Ltd.	Eye Physicians
Eyecare Optical	Eye Plastic Surgery
Eyecare Opticians	Eye Shoppes
Eyecare Physicians and Surgeons	Eye Specialists
Eyecare Vision Centers	Eye Surgeons
Eye Center	Eye to Eye Vision Center
Eye Clinic	Eye & Vision Care, Ltd.
Eye Consultants	Eyewear, Ltd.
Eye Diagnostic & Surgery Center	Eyecare Vision Center
Eye Fashion Factory	Eye Vision Center, Inc.
Eyeglass Vision Center	Eyeglasses To Go
Eye Healthcare, Inc.	Eyewear Loft
Eye Healthcare of St. Louis	

And that is in addition to those firms starting with "Vision" and "Opt-this-or-that," not to mention contact lenses. How in the world can the proprietors of these places expect to establish an identity? My father set an example. Most people didn't even know his first name; he was always "Dr. Koetting." It may seem a bit ostentatious, but I have followed suit in a good many ways, not to emphasize the "doctor" so much as to give people a chance to ask, "Oh, the contact lens doctor?" Or, "What kind of a doctor?" Either one is a pretty good way to tell people what you do.

As I said earlier, our advertising slogan was "When people in St. Louis think of contact lenses, they think of The Koetting Associates." It was not always true, of course, but a good many people did. And when I am introduced, more often than not, someone will relate my name to that practice. To have a name that is recognized in your community, one must first have a recognizable name.

Get Famous for Doing Something

Espouse a cause? Sure, as long as it's not too controversial. There are hundreds of worthy groups in every city just looking for a volunteer (Levoy 1966). It will take a while, so don't count on becoming the official spokesperson at your first meeting. But, sooner than you think, you will find there are unwanted high-profile jobs in just about every organization. No one wants to chair benefit parties nor accept the position of development director; yet, these people are often called upon for pictures and interviews, and their names appear on countless mailings. Try to find a group with a paid executive director who will do most of the work and make you look good.

Amateur sports figures from bowling teams to senior olympics get a disproportionate share of publicity via the sports pages. If you are not a jock, forget it, but don't overlook the possibility of combining business with pleasure.

Patron of the Arts

Well, I'm not a jock, so I had to look for something else. My PR consultant suggested community recognition by association with artistic endeavors. Our practice started with program ads: we sponsored symphony programs. I've held positions on several gallery boards, raised funds for the music conservatory, and made a lot of influential friends in the process.

While recovering from heart surgery in 1980, I took a university course in purchasing art. The instructor advised learning all one can about a very narrow field and making purchases within those limits. Local contemporary works seemed to fill the requirement, so my collection began.

Our office was previously decorated with "sofa art"—paintings that caused people who didn't know anything about art to say, "Isn't that pretty?" The transition was easy. I simply started taking pictures down one at a time and replacing them to build a collection. I even had a catalog printed (Figure 9.1). The next step involved sponsoring art shows and guaranteeing sales by making "purchase awards."

Without any real technical expertise, I've stuck to impressionistic and abstract works because these contemporary art forms are judged mostly by emotions, so the purchaser can make decisions based on likes or dislikes. (Besides, no one knows whether you are right or wrong.)

Your local artists are probably no worse than average, and a purchase will support culture in the community. You can use their creativity to enjoy and decorate your home and office at generally moderate prices.

Go to local juried exhibits and buy winners if they appeal to you. Talk to the artists, ask why, and get an explanation of the work. When your office walls are filled, start giving items to charity auctions. When someone asks how to get started, I usually suggest that if all else fails, take a course or read a book. Appreciation will come with experience.

Be a Joiner

Service clubs, country clubs, lodges, and church groups—I don't have to tell you what they are. The goal-oriented professional soon learns to

Figure 9.1 Patron of the arts. If you are going to support art in your community, it helps to let people know about it. This simple catalog identifies works in the office, and local artists are appreciative when their works are included.

have fun in the company of community-opinion-molders. The wisdom of Ben Franklin included something to the effect that falling in love with a *rich* woman takes no more effort than falling in love with a poor one. Learn to enjoy being with people who are potential patients. A young optometrist I know built a successful practice on the simple premise that he would never eat lunch alone.

Politics

And then there is the political arena. If most leaders in your town belong to the same party, stand up and be counted by all means! Avoid factions, and when you support politicians, try to back the winners.

Your community may be one in which one party is consistently elected and constantly in control, so there is no danger in affiliating yourself with that group. You can then become quite influential by forming a small business organization, a neighborhood improvement association, or some other type of politically oriented group devoted to the specific interests of members. Putting yourself in this position gives you access to incumbents, and you get to know promising new candidates for some all-important "connections."

In his somewhat sleazy book, *The Greedy Bastard's Business Manual*, R.H. Morrison suggested another way to reach a political power button (Morrison 1981). His realistic advice on selecting a new lawyer could be quite practical for a new practitioner.

During an election year, look over the names of young attorneys seeking a political office and engage one to handle some legal matters for you: collections, a new lease, or whatever. If the attorney loses the election, you have still made contact with an aggressive young lawyer, and if you are satisfied with the work, you can continue. On the other hand, if the lawyer wins the election, you have a good attorney plus a fine political connection. A win-win situation.

Media recognition, from backing a successful candidate or being appointed to a panel or commission, quite naturally follows. Fame by association is often a relatively simple matter. Access to the local power structure may even be attainable without a serious investment of your time or money.

Get Serious About Your Looks

It's been a long time since I read John Malloy's *Dress for Success*, but one story has stayed with me (Malloy 1975). It concerned a study of some sort conducted by psychology students at a university. The test was simple enough. A person dressed in typical workingman's clothing was stationed by the revolving door entrance to a large building. Timing himself to reach the door at the precise moment when someone else wished to enter, he created a situation where one of the parties had to step back. About 95% of the time, people shoved ahead of the blue-collared subject.

Then the test was repeated using the same door and the same person. Only this time he was well dressed in a tailored business suit. The numbers were exactly reversed. People stepped back away from the revolving door to allow this well-dressed person first entry. I do not know whether the results were statistically significant, but a lot of silk ties, white shirts, and copies of Malloy's book have been sold. I was sold too.

I agree with Linda Miles, who, when writing in *Optometric Management*, decried doctors who have the misconception that they shouldn't look too successful because patients may think their fees are too high (Miles 1990). A doctor who doesn't dress well will have a negative effect on the practice. Not only does it turn away quality patients who are sensitive to "details" but dressing poorly also creates a poor self-image and a lack of respect from the staff.

Self-image, says Miles, is directly reflected in fee schedules. Poor self-image and low fees go hand in hand. For men, she recommends a dress shirt and tie, dress slacks, an impeccable lab coat, and quality leather shoes. Women should wear quality suits, blouses, dresses, and accessories that have a professional business look.

Staff Too

And how about the rest of your staff? Your patients may notice many things about your office when they first enter, but their first impressions will be formed by what your employees are wearing. Of course there are two sides to the uniform issue. The opposition probably started somewhere during the 1970s. Some believe uniforms are degrading, sexist, and a restraint of personal expression. So why should your personnel wear them in the first place?

Let's start with identity. You *can* tell the players without a scorecard, and patients will recognize those persons wearing uniforms as staff members. More importantly, a uniform immediately converts the wearer into an authority figure. We don't expect an assistant to push people around, of course, but psychologists tell us that patients will accept instruction and advice more readily from someone dressed for the job. Uniforms are traditional in professional practices. Well-made, attractive career apparel boosts morale, makes a favorable impression on patients, and provides a genuine "status symbol" for an optometric aide. It shows that the person is on the health-care team and an important part of the doctor's practice.

Well-known practice management expert Harriett Stein observes that simply wearing a uniform is not enough. Part of your dress-code policy should include the care that is taken of an employee's appearance. This means clean hair, combed and nicely styled; uniforms professionally laundered and pressed; shoes cleaned and polished; tasteful makeup and jewelry, etc. Hands should be clean, and chipped nail polish avoided (Stein suggests it is probably best to use clear nail polish anyway).

Mustaches and beards need to be very well groomed, looking neat and clean. Those without beards must be clean shaven.

Long-sleeve shirts are a good rule for both males and females. Pants ought to be dress fabric or wool combinations. Polyester may be OK if it's new, says Stein, but like wool or silk, it tends to get shiny spots when worn out. And, she is strongly against white slacks in any fabric because they are very revealing and usually unattractive when viewed from the rear. Having a clearly defined dress policy for an office can help maintain that all-important image while instilling pride in the personnel.

If you want to dress for success, spend your time before you spend your money, experts tell us. Because a full wardrobe of "power" suits and outfits can cost thousands of dollars, buying proper clothes ought to be considered an investment.

My own tailor, Savile Row's David Shockley, believes the most important step you can take prior to making a substantial investment starts with reading self-help books and/or a serious consultation with your tailor (Graves 1989). Fewer and fewer salespeople are making retail clothing a career, which means there won't be many knowledgeable persons in your department store.

Like specialty contact lens fitting, "wardrobe consultants" are popping up to fill the void. After a tailor has sized up a client, the next step involves thinking about a budget. Women's fashions change dramatically from year to year, but men's clothing is generally resistant to drastic swings. In both cases, though, the color of a suit is important for the professional. As a general rule, the darker the suit, the more authority is conveyed. Tailors seem to agree that a man's full wardrobe should contain a minimum of five suits, one for each business day, as well as a couple of blazer and slack combinations and sport coats for less formal wear. Of the standard recommended 12 shirts, 100% cotton is usually suggested because it holds dye better, the colors are sharper, and the material breathes so that the wearer is cooler in summer and warmer in the winter. Ties ought to be 100% silk. Business suits are always appropriate for women. Having a stylish and coordinated spectacle frame may seem obvious to many readers, but my invisible monovision contact lenses have been major practice builders for more than a quarter century.

Lab Coats

So what should the doctor wear while seeing patients? Many feel the traditional lab coat or a jacket (not necessarily white) shows an interest in hygiene that is appropriate in the health-care professions. Others disagree, suggesting that a conventional business wardrobe is appropriate and not so snobbish. There is much to be said for both points of view, but I prefer a compromise. A light-colored blazer coordinated with the color of other office uniforms suggests the best of both worlds. It shows that the doctor doesn't just wear street clothes when caring for patients, without implying a disregard for fashion and proper appearance.

Your Image on Paper

I try never to mail a news release or article without including a head-and-shoulders high-contrast portrait. Notice in your own newspaper how those little one-paragraph business news items stand out when they are accompanied by a picture.

The media loves them, and directory publishers insist on up-to-date portraits. But how many of us have a good copy ready and waiting when the need arises?

You're on the phone with the program chairman who asked you to speak before his group. Just before hanging up, the chairman says, "By the way, we're going to be doing press releases about your talk. Could you send us a recent photograph?" Be prepared!

Professional photographers tell me they are appalled at the stuff they see in publicity shots: tired things from the family album, cropped photos taken from a group, security badge Polaroids, and the ever-popular pose standing in front of a brick wall squinting against the sun. The ready availability of cameras that will do just about everything for you has obscured the need for a professional photographer.

If it's been 4 to 5 years since your last sitting, now is the time to show you are getting better, not older. Know how the photograph will be used. A good quality black-and-white will be preferred for newspapers, brochures, or magazines 90% of the time. Remember that when the picture is printed, whites can only be as white as the paper, so a photo will never look as good in a newspaper as it will in a brochure. Color photographs will work, however, if the subject is sharp, clear, and crisp. Snapshots of any kind almost always reproduce poorly.

Size is also important. Often a wallet-size photo can be used, because its width almost matches that of a newspaper column. If the photo is to be part of a full-page ad, though, you'll want to submit a much larger print, such as an 8 × 10. A good rule of thumb is that it's always better to reduce the size than to enlarge it for publication.

While it may seem obvious, be sure to select a portrait photographer. Calling around and asking for prices won't help either. Take the time to visit a couple of studios and see the work on display. Be sure that the photographer knows how the final product will be used, and if on the day of your appointment you don't feel well or are overly tired, don't hesitate to reschedule. If you don't feel your best, you won't look your best. Your publicity portrait will say a lot about you before you will have a chance to say a word.

A Touch of Class

Without knowing anything about your community, it's a safe guess that civic leaders don't drive to the country club in a rusty pickup on Saturday night—their public image demands more "class." Some things that portray class are self-evident, but we may forget they are also important. Pay attention to detail down to the tips of your shoes. That last point may seem a bit trivial, but I am reminded of a local community leader I met a few years back. Ed was not a picky person. He was gregarious, outgoing, and willing to give anyone a fair hearing. Still, he subjected every salesperson to his personal test. He scrutinized the shoe heels of each person who called on him.

"Run-down heels," Ed told me, "indicate two things. First, the individual is indifferent to small details and probably won't watch the way in which his accounts are being handled. Moreover, there is a strong possibility that the worn-out footwear results from financial problems, indicating that his other customers feel the same way about him." The look of class is missing.

Security in one's appearance provides that confidence that goes hand in hand with class. You know what you are doing—so certain of yourself that patients can *feel* your self-assurance. You build a rapport with people you want to reach by radiating what *you* think you are.

Have your surroundings reflect your taste. The choices you make regarding office decor, magazines, furniture, background music, art on the walls, the automobile you drive, etc., can all communicate class. And that is a part of your image in the community.

Climb the ALPs

It takes time, but the Achievers, Leaders, and those with a high Profile have the most successful practices in the eye-care field. Success certainly does come to those who look successful.

10

Some Other Things You Should Know

The One-Minute What?

A couple of years ago there was a rash of books—the One-Minute-This-That-Or-The-Other—patterned after *The One-Minute Manager* (Blanchard and Johnson 1982). These books made light of a few things that really aren't quite so easy. Practice management may well be as challenging and complex as the practices of optometry, medicine, or law, but how would you like to put your skull in the hands of a one-minute brain surgeon?

The quick fix, the too-simple solution (relying entirely on the book), has no more place in your office than in the operating room or courthouse. Management is serious business.

Excellence in any profession cannot be achieved overnight. You learn the basics in school. You sharpen your skills in the practice of your profession. And, if you mean to excel, you keep up with the new thoughts and ideas by reading and attending seminars. *Running* your office requires the same dedication.

Making Better Use of Your Time

"Time is money" may not have been original with Benjamin Franklin, but he generally gets credit for this very appropriate observation. It's been many years since "the tyranny of the urgent" slipped into my vocabulary after reading Alec MacKenzie's *Time Trap* (Mackenzie 1990). We all tend to waste that very valuable commodity, time, on seemingly important pressing matters that aren't worth it. From Peter Drucker to Ross Weber, there is no shortage of advice for gaining control of your time. Each system has strengths and weaknesses, but everyone seems to like a list-making approach.

☐ ☐ ☐ ☐ ☐ **Making the Best Use of Time**

More than 60 years ago, management consultant Ivy Lee gave his famous advice. Responding to a request from Charles Schwab, then chairman of Bethlehem Steel Company, for assistance in time management, Lee suggested the following:

1. Every evening, list the six most important tasks for the next day in order of priority.
2. Every morning, work on your list sequentially, finishing each item before beginning the next.
3. At the end of the day, tear up the list and start over.

Other advice may be more sophisticated, but Lee's is almost good enough for me. In planning a work day, I make up two basic lists: a comprehensive long-range master program and a specific one covering that day. The master list covers everything I have to do, big or little, right away or in 6 months. It quantifies the workload.

To use it you must distribute and schedule the items on it so they actually get done. Review it daily, delete anything unnecessary or finished, and break down complicated tasks into components so you can schedule each one.

The daily list, like Ivy Lee's, should be drawn up late in the afternoon, ready for you to face in the morning with your patient schedule. Keeping it short prevents the paralysis that arises when the workload seems unmanageable. Take an extra couple of seconds to rank them 1, 2, or 3 according to the urgency.

Postal Problems

And then there's the mailbag! Life might have been simpler without Gutenberg or Xerox, but there is not much we can do about it. Your practice, if you let it, will be buried by paper. The Postal Service brings out the little kid in all of us, and this fascination leads to a dangerous disregard for priorities. I like Stephanie Winston's TRAF technique (Winston 1983). She says managing the paper you receive lies in decision-making and processing.

There are two things you can do with stuff on your desk. You can avoid managing it by leaving it there to gather dust (fingering and rereading it innumerable times), or you can TRAF it. TRAF is an acronym for four decisions you must make about each piece of mail. You can *Toss* it in the wastebasket, *Refer* it to someone else, *Act* on it, or *File* it. To put it another way, after the dog, man's next best friend is the wastecan.

A decade or two ago when I was active in the volunteer structure of the American Optometric Association, we experienced a major management policy change that applied to my own office: Do not save any correspondence that will not serve a definite need in the foreseeable future. The same for unread periodicals: If you don't have time to read them now, where will you get it when the next issues arrive? That "action" basket on your desk is not a file. TRAF everything.

☐ ☐ ☐ ☐ ☐ Efficient Filing

Computers have changed our approach to patient files, but every office keeps some hard copy. Although photographs and signatures are now electronically storable, I really don't know anyone who has a totally paperless office. It seems safe to say you have a lot of case records on hand. After visiting a good many practices I've made some observations:

1. Vertical filing is more efficient and looks better than drawers.
2. Keep records out where patients can see them and be impressed by the number. (If you're just starting in practice, be sure you have plenty of file space but leave the doors closed on all empty shelves.)
3. Use color-coded labels so anything out of place will show up immediately.
4. Assign patient ID numbers, and integrate everything with your computer.
5. Open vertical files form a marvelously efficient acoustic surface. Use them to deaden sound in your business office.

How Long Should You Keep Records?

Unfortunately, there is no good answer. You cannot rely on a malpractice statute of limitations as a guideline. The running of the statute may be delayed, for example, because of a patient's minority or some injury claim traceable to your action many years before. Also, there is no limit to how far Medicare may go back in auditing your records. Furthermore, the treatment of any patient makes retention of the records advisable even when there is no specific legal requirement to do so.

The purists will tell you that information ought to be retained throughout a patient's lifetime and even 3 years after death.

Saving old records need not be onerous. Go through the exercise no more than once a year, and remember, although storage consumes a great deal of space, you don't have to keep files on the premises. Rent self-storage space, or use a business archives service. Somewhere in between, cost-wise, is micro-film service.

The storage of computer database information presents a challenge that is met in a variety of ways. Keeping back-up disks or tapes is becoming more practical and is less bulky than retention of hard-copy records. On the other hand, I've heard more than a few complaints from optometrists who have changed computer systems only to encounter endless difficulties when they attempted to transfer information. Critical materials should probably be stored in printout form until the day one feels certain that any new equipment will be compatible with ease of transfer.

Some Thoughts on Inventory

Successful inventory management involves simultaneously attempting to balance the costs of inventory with its benefits. Most optometrists fail to fully appreciate the true cost of carrying inventory. This not only includes the direct investment in storage, insurance, taxes, etc. but also the cost of money. Total cost may easily amount to 15% or 20% of your gross annually. Furthermore, tied-up capital places quite a strain on the bottom line.

Turnover

When commonly used, a simple measure of managerial performance is the inventory turnover rate. This value gives a rough guideline by which performance may be measured and goals set. Lens inventory turnover is calculated by dividing the annual lens purchase expense by the value of lenses on hand. This might be any figure from 1.0 to 20.0, but in a well-run office, the turnover will be about 3.0 to 5.0. A high-service practice that attempts to keep lenses for virtually all emergencies may have a turnover ratio as low as 1.5.

In recent years, two approaches have become popular in inventory management: material requirements planning (MRP) and just-in-time (JIT) are the commonly used terms.

Material requirements planning involves computerized ordering of components for assembly and is generally beyond the scope of optometric offices. Just-in-time inventory management is an approach that works to eliminate inventories rather than optimize them. This is accomplished by reducing lead times so that small lots may be ordered and suppliers make more frequent deliveries, even though pricing is based on large orders. "Just common sense," you say? It sure is!

☐ ☐ ☐ ☐ ☐ **Checking Up On Your Checks**

Watch the nickels and dimes, the old saying goes, and the dollars will take care of themselves. Well, maybe. Just the same when it comes to checks. Here are ten bits of information that can't do any harm:

1. *Avoid genuine fraud.* A good many of your patients will be referred by mutual acquaintances. That's good! If you are really dealing with a con artist, you probably don't have a chance, but there is a disreputable fringe that will take advantage only if you make it very easy for them. Get complete information for your records: social security numbers and addresses and phone numbers, both at home and at work.

2. *Cut cash loss, intentional or otherwise.* Except for well-established patients (and even then it is not wise), don't cash personal checks or give change when the face amount is greater than your bill. If you must, set a definite limit and be sure that your staff understands that the accountant is to blame—"I'd certainly like to cash your check, Mrs. Jones, but our accounting firm has set a rule that it must be for the exact amount of our service."

3. *Don't change your name.* An error on a check may go unnoticed until you are ready to deposit it. Perhaps your name has been misspelled or is incorrect for some other reason. When this happens, the best procedure is to endorse the check exactly as written and then add your proper endorsement beneath it. When a name is long, unusual, or difficult to spell, this might be a frequent occurrence. Asking patients to leave it blank for a rubber stamp eliminates errors and saves time for everyone.

4. *When checks aren't signed.* If you notice that a patient has neglected to sign a check, your bank will probably allow you to deposit it with a guarantee that you'll take it back if protested. In this case, simply write "over" on the line where the signature should appear. Then, on the back of the check, type "Lack of signature, guaranteed" with your regular endorsement. If the missing signature is an honest oversight, the patient certainly will not protest.

5. *Rubber checks shouldn't rebound.* Occasionally you will have one returned for "nonsufficient funds." When this happens, your assistant should call a responsible person at once. The "NSF" notice is rarely a surprise. Run it through again if directed to do so, but advise the person that bank charges will be applied to the patient's account.

6. *Trust the Postal Service.* When a patient tells you "the check is in the mail" and several days have passed, be tactful but suspicious. Under federal

law, if debtors "stop payment" on checks at your request, they can deduct the cost of the stop-payment from the amount they owe you. Just ask for another one, and assure the patient that you will return the duplicate check if it ever reaches your office.

7. *Watch out for thieves.* As a general rule, burglars don't want checks. Even so, a daily bank deposit will avoid theft of any kind.

8. *Control repeat offenders.* Your assistants must learn to smile and murmur sweetly, "I am sorry, Mrs. Jones, our accountant has asked me to have you pay by cash or with a money order. I hope you understand. Also, we will need the entire amount before your lenses can be ordered."

9. *Be cautious about bankruptcy.* When dealing with a party who has previously filed bankruptcy, that individual may not care about the stigma and knows how inexpensive the procedure can be. Remember, under current law, a bankrupt no longer has to wait 7 years to file again.

10. *Keep your eyes open.* Establish a policy of bonding every person in your office who handles funds. This is just good business and must be done regardless of how much you trust your employees.

When You're Talking Big Money

Finding a bank to provide financial services for your práctice is more complicated than choosing a personal banker. Business banking requires a hard look toward future needs and the bank's willingness to help the practice grow. Determine which banking services are most important to your operation.

- Does your practice require more than a commercial checking account? How about loan options, payroll, cash management, and direct deposit?
- Do you anticipate the practice's needs exceeding the lending limits that will be placed on it? Changing banks in midstream can be inconvenient and expensive, so try to make an accurate assessment.
- Have you developed a relationship with the branch manager or other person who will be handling the account?

It is important to be comfortable with the people who will be handling your money. Schedule time to sit down with your banker and talk about your practice and hopes for its future. And, you must work with the bank, completing paperwork and making accessible any pertinent information that will make the job easier.

□ □ □ □ □ Six Ways to Get a Loan

Financing for a small business is hard to find. The federal government has drastically reduced the number of small business loans once available to fledgling entrepreneurs, while banking institutions remain reluctant to invest in risky ventures. Providing potential lenders with an analysis of your working capital and collateral and a business plan have become very important. This is not a book on start-up procedure, so we will narrow it down to suggestions most often offered by accountants.

1. Attempt to secure a commercial loan.
2. Banks prefer to finance businesses with a track record of 3 to 5 years in existence. They will ask to see at least 3 years of personal tax returns and 3 to 5 years of financial records from the business. Have them available.
3. They also prefer persons who can provide collateral and some of their own capital, especially when the potential borrower has no previous background information.
4. Consider equity financing, an arrangement where someone finances your practice in exchange for co-ownership. This is not desirable but may be necessary.
5. Determine your chances of acquiring financing from non-banking institutions. This is equally undesirable, but friends, neighbors, or relatives may be able to provide the capital.
6. Look into loan programs sponsored by the Small Business Administration (SBA). The SBA will guarantee bank loans under two programs. Both guarantee 90% of a loan that doesn't exceed $750,000, and the term may be as long as 25 years. The average amount is $125,000.

   The first program is the Preferred Lender Program which is made through one of the few banks the SBA has deemed a preferred lender. These institutions can make loans without Administration approval. Criteria are similar to standard commercial loans.

   The second program is the Certified Lender Program. Again, the would-be borrower applies through the bank. This time, however, information concerning the loan application is submitted for approval to the Administration, which should respond within 3 working days.

If you have interest in either of these programs, a request to the Small Business Administration will produce more information than you might imagine.

Lease or Buy

Should you buy or lease equipment for your office? The decision is more complex than it might seem. To begin with, there are two types of leases: finance and operating. They are quite different.

A *finance lease* involves monthly payments for a certain number of years and the right to buy the equipment for a fixed (often nominal) amount. Your monthly payments plus the fixed payment at the end will have fully paid for the equipment, as well as the interest on the deferred payments.

These leases are by far the easiest to evaluate. If you are considering a $20,000 instrument on a 4-year finance lease, you can ask your local bank how much it would cost for such a loan and compare the bank's offer with the monthly lease payments.

An *operating lease* is a true lease, rather than a financing device, because the equipment goes back to the lessor when you have reached the end of the term. What your money has bought is simply the use of the equipment. This type of lease may be especially appropriate if you are obtaining some of the newer computerized instruments or computers, because these generally become obsolete relatively soon and their resale value at the end of the leasing term is likely to be low. On the other hand, payments will probably be higher because the company has less time in which to generate income.

When you purchase a piece of equipment or if you obtain a financing lease, you can write off most of the purchase price within the first few years. (Under 1991 laws, you can deduct the first $10,000 of equipment purchase in the first year, even before calculating the depreciation deduction.) With an operating lease, however, you can only deduct the lease payments as made. For most optometrists, therefore, a purchase of a finance lease will generally make more sense than an operating lease when it comes to paying taxes.

How to Pick an Accountant

Sound financial and tax planning is the foundation of good practice management. Even with a good computer package in your office, you still need an accountant's help, because accountants do more than handle taxes.

A *certified public accountant* (CPA) can devise an accounting system that best serves your practice's needs; tackle accounting aspects of your business problems; help organize, plan, and monitor financial activities; and create a computerized records system geared toward keeping your books in order.

Additionally, a CPA can offer advice on financing, inventories, cost credits, and collection, while preparing your tax returns and recommending strategies they believe will save money for you.

If you are looking for a new accountant, you have probably already received recommendations from your lawyer and small business owners in your community. If the choice has been narrowed down to one or two, you are ready for an interview. It helps to begin with a systematic process:

1. Outline your evaluation criteria.
2. Choose reasonable candidates for your needs.
3. Interview them one at a time until you feel comfortable with the selection.
4. Verify credentials or references.
5. Make your selection, and be ready to take advice.

The "Big Six"—type firms have a greater cadre of people with business experience, but they tend to be geared toward the "bigger is better" philosophy, so small accounts are often internally perceived as somewhat less desirable clients. The local or regional firms generally offer a wider range of the fundamental services you will require. They also provide a greater continuity of staffing, which avoids a lot of time otherwise spent annually teaching new accountants about your practice and allow you to develop a stronger rapport with the people serving your office. The cost is generally less because billing rates are lower due to vast reduction in overhead and national office costs.

Accountants' fees depend on the number of services they are asked to perform. By keeping good records, for instance, you can save your accountant time and yourself money.

How to Find the Right Legal Advice

While relaying the story of an automobile accident, a friend of mine also summed up the major problem we face in selecting a lawyer. Following his mishap, the insurance company had paid the medical bills without question but balked at an item to replace lost earnings during the month he spent recuperating. His attorney came through with an outstanding job of convincing the insurors to pay the disability claim. Two years later, he enthusiastically asked the same lawyer to draw up some business contracts and was woefully disappointed. There are, he found, specialties within the legal profession, just as we have them in our own field.

For that very reason, I've always felt comfortable paying a little more and dealing with a firm large enough to include a variety of specialists. You need legal advice if you are

- organizing your practice as a partnership or corporation
- signing contracts of any kind
- buying, selling, or leasing real estate
- seeking advice on matters involving employees
- drawing up a pension plan or asking advice on insurance
- occasionally in need of copyright protection
- drawing up your will

□ □ □ □ □ How to Recognize a Good Lawyer

- *Knowledgeable and experienced.* Hopefully someone who has "been there before" when a difficult situation arises.
- *Accessible.* Your phone calls should be returned right away, not a day or two later.
- *Responsive.* When you need a quick opinion or immediate advice, a good lawyer will give you a prompt and forthright answer.

And, just in case you're wondering whether anyone rates lawyers, they do. The *Martindale-Hubbell Law Directory* does just that. You can probably borrow one from a law school library (most likely for a fee if you are not a student there) and learn a great deal about your attorney's scholastic background, professional history, and community activities. The *Directory* also provides descriptions of specialties within each firm. With the rating system, "legal ability" may be graded A (very high), B (high to very high), or C (fair to high). A general recommendation, based on confidential information from lawyers and judges in the area, is also published with the ratings.

Although your gut feeling may be the best indication of which firm or attorney to choose, never be afraid to ask about fees. Does the same per-hour charge apply if an associate does the work rather than a partner? Must a retainer be completely paid up-front, or can partial payments be made? Does the firm or individual lawyer only get paid if a case is won? In many larger cities there are law firms that even specialize in health-care practices, so don't wait until you are in trouble to get acquainted.

Location, Location, Location

Marketing certainly includes being in the "right place at the right time." Although the contact lens field is changing rapidly, a few fundamentals still apply. For example, a practice limited to contact lenses is risky when the number exceeds one practice per drawing area of 350,000 persons. On the positive side, people will travel many miles, passing other offices, to visit a specialty practice.

□ □ □ □ □ Ways to Recognize the "Right" Location

In 1963, Harold J. Ashe, listed the significant factors in choosing an optometric location. They have not changed.

1. Study the kind, volume, and timing of prospective-patient traffic passing the site.
2. Relate this to the habits of prospective patients regarding the services you will offer.
3. Seriously study the convenience of the location relative to streets and expressways.
4. Be sure adequate parking facilities are available.
5. Check into public transportation. (In a specialty practice, this also includes airports.)
6. Look carefully at other professional, retail, and service establishments in the area.
7. Evaluate the probable cost of practicing there relative to estimated earnings.
8. Be sure the site is available.

Your Prospective Location Should be P.A.I.D.

Does it have The Big Four?

Prestige
Accessibility
Identity
Design

Even if you're buying an established practice, these same rules apply. After looking over the books, you should be able to answer "yes" to each of the following questions:

- Is this a good working practice with an established pattern of growth, or was the previous owner living on the reputation of years gone by?
- Does the office meet the PAID formula, or was it successful only because of the former owner's skill and personality?
- If the office is not physically what I would like for it to be, will the patients follow me to a new location and, if so, where?

□ □ □ □ □ **Fourteen Ways to Design an Efficient Examining Room**

In the process of franchising some offices, and having moved my own a half dozen times, I've seriously considered and laid out well over a hundred examining rooms before reaching what I consider the ideal combination. Here it is (Figure 10.1):

1. Make floor space do double duty by using a mirror. The limited psychological advantage of a 20-foot refracting lane is certainly offset by the high cost of office space. If the mirror is large enough (at least 3 × 4 feet) and of good quality, patients will never know the difference.

2. The ideal examining room is 11 feet long. With a chair placed so that the patient's head is 2 feet from the back wall, the cornea-to-chart distance will be exactly 20 feet.

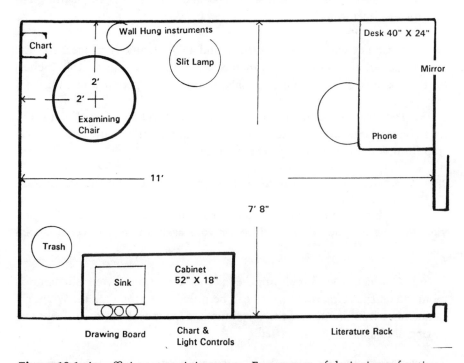

Figure 10.1 An efficient examining room. Forty years of designing refracting ranges led to this 11′ × 7′8″ format. Perimetry, keratometry, fundus photography, etc. are performed in another room, because that equipment needn't be tied up during the whole of a patient's visit. Doors should never be placed where the doctor or assistant must walk in front of the patient. The sink and writing surface can be reached without taking an extra step.

3. The entry door to an examining room should be on the patient's right side so the doctor or technician will never have to cross in front of the patient.

4. The bottom edge of the mirror should be high enough to prevent patients from seeing a reflection of anything below face level during the examination. The lower edge ought to be at least 50 inches above the floor to prevent the self-conscious clothing- and posture-checking that is common to all humans facing their own reflections.

5. The projector is least likely to be blocked when it is placed on the patient's left side. This is also inconvenient, so you should have a remote control.

6. A nearpoint chart light and reading lamp mounted on a refracting unit is always in the way. Remove it and mount a spotlight or two strategically placed on the examining room ceiling.

7. All illumination controls should be on the patient's right (doctor's left) for efficient operation.

8. A cabinet with working surface and a small sink is an ideal fixture. It must be tall enough (about 54 inches) and long enough (about 48 inches) for the doctor and/or assistant to make notes on the patient's record.

9. The ideal examining room width is about 7 feet 8 inches. Wider is OK if you have a large refracting unit, but you should never be more than a single step from your writing area to the phorpter.

10. A telephone/intercom in every room saves steps for the entire staff.

11. Each examining room should have a small desk and chair. This provides seating for guests and a place for your assistant to go over financial matters.

12. You can save 3 to 5 minutes per examination if your slit lamp is mounted on the refracting unit or can be rolled up to the patient. When patients move from instrument to instrument, a great deal of time is lost readjusting chairs and getting settled.

13. Have a coat room available and use it. Outer garments in examining rooms waste space and create confusion as patients move from one room to another.

14. Employ some sort of signal system so that you and the staff will know which rooms are occupied and the order in which patients should be seen.

11 □ □ □
□ □ □
□ □ □
□ □ □

Contact Lens Replacement

In the world of contact lens replacement, things were never so straightforward as in days of old when Henry Ford painted all cars black. But, for at least a generation, the matter was a lot less complex than it is today. Prepaid continuing care really fitted neatly in one of three pigeon holes:

1. *Pure service.* No special deals on lenses, just prepaid service.
2. *Lens replacement.* Lower prices for those who paid a fee in advance.
3. *Combination.* Some service, reduced lens prices, and, occasionally, discounted supplies.

How simple it was! Those days are behind us now, although some of the basics still apply.

The Way We Were

No one calls it contact lens insurance anymore. It really never was *insurance*, of course, because by definition that would involve the risk of losing money, and *service agreements* or *policies* were never designed that way. In fact, there were so many approaches to the matter, it sometimes seemed most were not designed at all.

Many optometrists, even those in price houses, strongly agreed that more emphasis should be placed on payment for professional care. Our office followed this philosophy so closely that the agreement didn't even cover lenses. We charged a fixed amount per year only for office visits, gambling on the experience that the average patient would return about two times annually. Refractions and eye health exams were extra.

It worked. The arrangement was profitable, and we dispensed replacement lenses at a competitive fee. Furthermore, each patient who renewed belonged to our practice for another year. Then came disposables and planned replacement programs.

These new concepts demanded two, and later three, types of service agreements. The situation was confusing to patients and doctors alike, but one fact remained abundantly clear: both parties wanted and benefitted from contractual arrangements.

The No Frills Approach

Some other practitioners placed emphasis on the bonding advantage of an agreement. Keep the up-front cost as low as possible, they reasoned, and charge deductibles. This seemed to offer the best of both worlds, or as Jerry Hayes, an expert in optometric marketing, put it, "No matter how much free service you've got built into your plan, it's much tougher to get a patient to renew at $50 with freebies than at $25 with all services a la carte."

Nevertheless, when consumers buy anything, they are looking for benefits, and in this case, they must at least perceive that the service agreement offers convenience and/or economy worthy of the expense. When a front-end charge is high, emphasis must go to convenience—"You won't have to worry about your eyes for another year, even if you are a little short of cash." Otherwise, low cost is a selling feature—"The agreement is only $30 and it will cover you all year long." Two schools of thought with a common thread!

□ □ □ □ □ Components of a Contact Lens Fee

Basic exam (may be covered by third party)

- refraction
- eye health exam
- etc.

Contact lens exam (rarely covered by third party)

- measurements
- observation of diagnostic lenses
- etc.

Dispensing and instructions (often combined with warranty or service agreement)

- dispensing observations
- instructions
- care kit

First lenses (frequently included with dispensing and initial warranty or service agreement)

- may be changed during initial wear period

Initial wear period/warranty or service agreement (usually 60, 90, or 180 days)

- office visits
- lens changes
- disposables or frequent replacement packs
- provision for refund

Replacement lenses

- charge for lenses
    or
- prepaid
    or
- conventional service agreement
    or
- covered by third party

Office visits

- charge for visit
    or
- included in service agreement
    or
- covered by third party (unusual)

Solutions

- cash sale
    or
- included in service agreement

Annual examination — eye health and refraction

- charge for exam
    or
- included in service agreement
    or
- paid by third party

Facts that Modify the Bottom Line

1. combinations of components
2. simple case (currently wearing lenses)
3. standard case
4. complex case — specialty lenses, extended wear, or cosmetic
5. frequency of lens replacement
6. variables in how much suppliers charge for lenses

Enter Disposables

A couple of years ago, Johnson & Johnson rocked the field. How could we tell patients to discard a lens after only a week or two? Most of us felt that people would make a six-pack last a lifetime because we didn't understand the "pantry principle."

What Your Grocer Knows

Suppose a typical consumer buys and uses an ordinary-size package of detergent and jar of peanut butter every month. And, suppose that while shopping this time that person purchases the giant economy box of detergent and the super family-size jar of peanut butter. Do you believe the consumer won't have to buy these items again next month?

Wrong! The big box will not last much longer than a small one. It's called the *pantry principle:* when people have a lot of anything, they tend to be less concerned about running out, perhaps even wasteful. Grocers have known that for years. It may be news to you because doctors seldom think that way.

There was much alarm when disposable lenses entered the marketplace. Critics contended that patients would not comply with instructions and predicted they would begin stockpiling. Now, several years later, experience indicates that people rarely have lenses left over when it's time to buy a new pack. The pantry principle continues to hold true. When consumers have a quantity of anything on hand, including contact lenses, they use it without restraint.

Contacts are easily replicated now. Clean lenses mean fewer red eyes, fewer complaints, and less professional time spent solving problems. Spare lenses mean fewer spoiled vacations, fewer mornings late for work, and fewer emergency trips to your office on Saturday afternoon. Everybody wins!

A Lesson from the Shoe Trees

I could probably make a similar parable with reference to almost any item of merchandise. This one came home quite forcefully not too long ago. I wanted to buy a pair of shoe trees for travel that would be lighter than the cedar-block type with which we are all familiar. Shopping for them was facilitated by browsing through the mountain of direct-mail catalogs that arrives on my desk every morning.

I quickly discovered something in common. A half dozen companies sold cedar shoe trees, and the price was amazingly consistent—about $16.50 for the merchandise plus $4.75 shipping and handling. Why doesn't someone just make the cheap, light-weight kind I am looking for? I wondered. Then one day I wandered into a local drugstore and found the shoe trees I wanted for $2.43. And the whole thing became very clear—only a high-volume, low-overhead establishment can justify selling anything for $2.43. Even at a 200% to 300% markup, the mail-order firms can't make enough at that price; nor can we survive on the profit from low-priced lenses alone. Packs must be part of a program that ensures total fees high enough to be worth the effort.

What Is Your Time Worth?

So you want to develop your own continuing service agreement. You want patients to return, you don't want it to be prohibitively costly, and, let's suppose for the moment, you also want to include contact lens–related office visits but no annual examinations or refractions. We will also disregard lens replacements for now.

1. Determine the number of minutes you have available each year. Simply multiply your working days by the average number of hours you see patients and again by the number of people you care for at the same time (examining chairs). Multiply again by 60 minutes.

For example, let's say you have two examining rooms and work 7 hours a day, 250 days a year.

$$250 \times 7 \times 2 \times 60 = 210,000 \text{ minutes}$$

2. Figure what it costs each minute you see a patient and add some reasonable net for yourself. This is another straightforward calculation. If

your annual overhead (exclusive of materials) is $80,000 and you expect to take home about $88,000, it works out this way:

$$\$80,000.00 + \$88,000.00 = \$168,000.00$$

$$\frac{210,000 \text{ minutes}}{\$168,000} = \$1.25 \text{ per minute}$$

The next steps will take a while longer. You will have to go through a few hundred records for accuracy, but it will be worth the effort.

3. Determine how many minutes of chair time are consumed by the average patient during certain key procedures. A 60-minute examination at $1.25 per minute ought to be billed at no less than $75. A 20-minute office visit at $1.25 per minute would be $25, etc.

4. How many times will you provide care during the 1-year life of a service agreement? Chances are it's not as often as you think. Even under disposable and frequent replacement programs, most people come in fewer than three times, and 2.6 visits is a pretty safe average.

$$2.6 \times \$25.00 = \$65.00$$

So, $65 per year might well be a fair, safe, and equitable charge. Add another $10 to cover the cost of printing and handling your service agreement, and you can't go wrong with a $75 policy if these figures fit your practice.

The Changing Field of Frequent Replacement

We optometrists are conscientious—that's good! But, we've spent a generation teaching patients that contact lenses should last forever, and that was dumb! When disposable lenses entered the marketplace, it was time to stop and ask, "How did we ever begin to violate so many principles of patient care and management while ignoring that all-American cornerstone of commerce: *planned obsolescence?*"

Ask providers in any other field, and you'll hear a thousand ways to make things wear out sooner—changing the style, improving the package, increasing the demand, etc. Yet, we've spent 20 years trying to clean deposits off of soft contact lenses.

In our dedication to provide patients with better service, we've extended the perceived lifespan of the material, leaving behind a trail of red eyes and itching lids.

By dispensing fewer lenses, we have placed ourselves in the awkward position of charging too much for contacts and too little for care. Our neverending effort to take the patient's side moved us to join them in blaming manufacturers whenever a given lens didn't meet our arbitrary standard of 2 years of useful life. "I'm sorry, this lens must be defective" or "I'll see if we can't get it cleaned up for you" became standard replies. It is no wonder that we charged so much when the patient finally got around to getting new ones.

Manufacturers introduced disposable lenses with advertising focused on convenience. When worn as intended, they eliminated the need for cleaning, disinfection, or storage. But the original intended use changed as negative reports about extended wear caused practitioner and consumer interest to wane. Since 1989, dispensers have responded by emphasizing daily wear with a 2-week life cycle, requiring maintenance just as before.

In fact, contact lens companies and dispensers now believe the enhanced comfort and health benefit attained by removing a lens daily and disposing of it after 2 weeks have replaced the solutions-saving benefit of 7-day extended wear as the key force driving lens sales.

Even though disposable contacts are somewhat disappointing in the overall market, they form an important part of the frequent replacement philosophy that has begun to catch on at long last.

Encouraging, too, is their percentage of use in independent practice. While it has been reported that chain retailers' sales of disposables were off 50% in 1990, disposable use increased substantially in the offices of private O.D.s. Convenience isn't the big thing any more. Practitioners have learned that clean lenses really do mean healthy eyes.

How Long Can You Wear a Lens?

Relating lens replacement charges to the length of a wearing period has never been practical, nor even completely candid. In the early days of "extended wear" there was some justification, because frequent monitoring and additional visits were mandatory. Also, the laboratory charge for lenses was occasionally higher.

That ended years ago. The cost of a lens has nothing to do with number of hours or days a patient chooses to wear it. Even the number of checkups per year has all but standardized, so why the fee differential?

A majority of patients seem to prefer a flexible schedule anyway. Recognizing the possible risks involved, they are perfectly willing to remove lenses when there is no particular reason for leaving them under a closed lid. While planned replacement programs have introduced some serious challenges to our fee schedules, this one can be put to rest at last.

Marketing the Idea One-on-one

"Why don't they just make lenses like they used to? I wore my old contacts for almost 2 years, but these new lenses are only good for 3 months, or 2 weeks, or 6 months, or whatever." That's a reasonable question, so hit it head-on.

Soft lenses are as good as they ever were. In fact, they are probably even better, but we've learned a lot about eye health during the last couple of years. You can start marketing replacement programs right now by telling every patient you see that current research has shown that people who change lenses more often have significantly fewer problems. Add a personal touch by telling them *you* have noticed fewer infections and less irritation when your patients replace lenses. I have a couple of stories to illustrate the point.

During World War II, and for a few years thereafter, it was assumed that a heavy intake of sodium chloride would avoid heat exhaustion. In the armed services, and on many jobs, people were literally forced to eat salt tablets. I gave this a great deal of thought while looking at that bland and tasteless hospital food after my bypass surgery. Can you imagine anyone recommending a high-salt diet nowadays?

There are plenty of other examples: cigarettes, asbestos, dioxin, and so many things we thought were OK. We know better now. Craig Norman, O.D., once suggested making the point by scaring patients with a series of photos showing dirty lenses and GPC (Giant Papillary Conjunctivitis). Do it any way you like, but don't apologize for bringing them the latest news.

☐ ☐ ☐ ☐ ☐ Seven Ways to Sell a Service Agreement

1. *Class.* Like anything else that is mailed from your office, printed material your patient receives is *you*. The policy is a contract (Figure 11.1). It assures the purchaser that your office will be there for a year, dependably providing quality care for some fairly substantial sum paid in advance. This is no place for a cheap print job. It must look *dependable*.

2. *Stress benefits.* Healthy eyes, reduced cost, convenience—patients will be worry-free for another year.

3. *Offer a comparison.* Make your computer pay off. Provide a summary of last year's activity. If you can't (or don't want to) base it on history, set up a hypothetical situation.

4. *Timely mailing.* Send the renewal notice and explanatory material about a month before an active agreement expires. If no response has been received by the renewal date, a second notice ought to be mailed without delay.

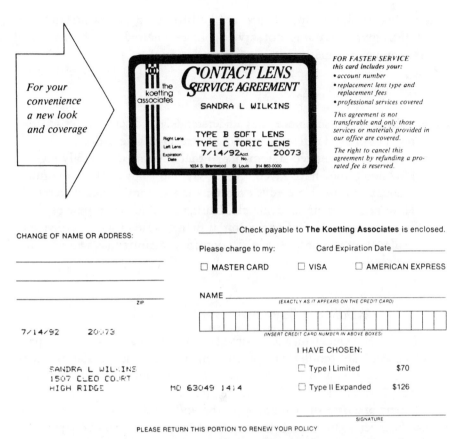

To help you determine which of our two service agreements is best for you, we have included a summary of your account history for the past year.

Figure 11.1 A service agreement form. The service agreement form places benefits before the patient. This multipurpose service agreement renewal form includes a new ID card and offers payments in the form of a credit card charge. More importantly, a summary of the previous year's activities makes the benefit clear to everyone.

5. *Make it painless.* Even your most affluent patients may have a cash-flow problem from time to time. We found that a surprising number of people would rather charge the renewal to MasterCard or VISA than to simply send a check. Enclosing a postage-paid addressed envelope also helps a lot. When the amount is substantial, you may wish to offer semiannual or even quarterly payments.

6. *Follow up.* A telephone call to delinquent policyholders serves two purposes: If some genuine problem exists, you certainly want to know about it;

on the other hand, some people just need a little push. In our practice, we consistently found the number of service policies renewed could be increased by 15% through telemarketing.

7. *Set the stage.*

- Talk it up. Be sure your staff understands and discusses the advantages of prepaid care each time a patient is in your office.
- Design computerized statements so that patients can readily see how much they have saved. (Never say "No charge." Show the full amount, and issue a credit, even for the most insignificant items.)
- Have printed material available. During an office visit, new patients nearing the end of the initial fitting period should receive an explanatory pamphlet in preparation for a mailing that will be coming soon.

A Dollar a Day?

How much for a four-pack? How much for a six-pack? Or a spare pair or a dozen? The proliferation of replacement plans and undulating prices defy specific advice. A high fee for service generally suggests a lower charge for lenses. Those that are replaced more often require less cleaning, etc., so a good many practitioners have adopted the *dollar-a-day* rule, balancing one against the other, so the average patient winds up spending about $350 per year.

Keep It Simple

How do you avoid using brand names or even talking about "astigmatic" or "extended-wear" lenses? I like to put them into categories based upon the replacement charge:

Type A	$25
Type B	$35
Type C	$50
Type D	$75
Type E	Special fee

In this way, any single lens or pack can be identified without referring to a list that looks more like an airline schedule. The computer bill simply states, "Type B" or "Type D," etc., with the appropriate charge. If a manufacturer's price changes substantially, the lens type may be altered accordingly.

Reordering and Inventory

The original concept was simple enough. The average optometrist who sold disposable lenses or participated in a frequent replacement program would be dispensing about 100,000 lenses a year. Storing that many could be challenge enough, while most practices wouldn't even be able to finance such an enormous inventory. Unfortunately, the suppliers' computer-generated, patient-based lens replacement system wasn't the right answer either.

Neither was the "just-in-time" (JIT) system of quarterly multi-pack deliveries in some cases. As Ronald Snyder, O.D., speaking from the practice of Drs. Solomon, Snyder, and Klein in Ft. Lauderdale, put it, "The system had limited success for several reasons: Variations in lifestyle resulted in some wearers needing additional lenses prior to their scheduled quarterly visits, while others were weeks and even months late; poor management of these orders occasionally resulted in the accumulation of excess inventory; and, frequently, quarterly office visits revealed the need for a change in power and/or parameter or discard cycle." On occasion, he said, financial, physiological, or metabolic reasons necessitated the discontinuance of disposable lenses or change to an alternative manufacturer.

Like many others, this optometric group discontinued JIT and is dispensing a single pair of lenses from the diagnostic set during an office visit if required. Multi-packs are then ordered and mailed to the patient to avoid further inconvenience.

For those people whose lens parameters do not change from visit to visit, they employ an alternative approach. Patients are simply advised to call the office and place an order for additional lenses when they have one or two unopened pairs remaining. Delivery of the new set is timed to coincide with routine examination visits. This same approach can obviously be applied to 1-month, quarterly, or semiannual replacement plans.

Serious Questions

1. *How long can we continue to combine fees for service and materials?* The days are just about over.
   - Simple spherical flexwear lenses are now available for about 80% of your patients. They are dependably replicated and really don't require a dispensing visit.
   - Price comparison of materials makes legitimate doctors appear to be "gouging" in the opinion of many patients.
   - People do recognize the value of professional service and are willing to pay for it. Many don't trust those who charge too little.

- An ever-increasing number of third-party providers demands separate fees for service and materials.

2. *How can we determine charges for replacement lenses?* Many suggest a handling charge or as little as 30% or 40% to the cost of materials. The days of 100% to 200% markup are over. (Besides, what is the value of a 200% markup on a $2.50 lens?)

3. *What about specialty lenses?* Patients needing toric lenses, bifocals, cosmetic tints, or even older thicker designs (yes, these still work better on some problem patients) are victims of the 80-20 rule. The cost of frequent replacement may be nearly prohibitive for some people. Hopefully, manufacturers will expand programs to include everyone.

4. *When should I begin suggesting a 2-week, 1-month, 3-month, or semi-annual replacement program to every patient?* NOW!

12 🔲🔲🔲
🔲🔲🔲
🔲🔲🔲

You and the Third Party

Strictly speaking, eye care involves two people: you and your patient. If someone else participates in any way, that is a "third party." We couldn't hope to cover all the possibilities in one chapter, but an overview is probably in order.

Optometry has had problems with the third-party system in general and major medical insurance programs in particular, in large part because of a communication failure. There is a myth that major medical insurance doesn't cover optometric service. The problem rises from the belief held by patients and insurers that optometrists merely perform routine vision examinations or contact lens–related activities. We have reinforced this misconception by the way we report patient encounters using a very limited set of diagnoses.

With the Medicare definition of optometrists as physicians for reimbursement purposes, state Freedom of Choice laws, and strong health maintenance organization (HMO) laws, there are no legal barriers to practicing and receiving adequate payment for medical optometry in most of the 50 states. The challenge to make insurers understand the medical nature of optometric services is ours. This requires us to understand the "medical care philosophy."

It is unfortunately true that third-party payment is rarely, if ever, adequate where contact lens service is concerned. (Some might argue this same frugality extends throughout the entire system.) In any event, we are facing at least four different fronts.

1. *Vision-care plans*
   Participating
   Nonparticipating
   In-house
2. *Governmental plans*
   Medicare
   Medicaid

State or local programs
  Aid to the blind
  Rehabilitation programs
  Etc.
3. *Conventional insurance*
  Contact lens insurance plans
  Accident, property loss, and liability
4. *Managed care systems*
  Preferred provider organizations (PPO)
  Individual practice associations (IPA)
  HMOs
  Etc.

□ □ □ □ □ Terms to Know When Dealing with a Third Party

alternative delivery systems (ADS)   Sometimes called managed care systems, they come in a wide variety of forms. See HMO, PPO, and limited service health care organizations.

capitation   A fixed amount paid to a provider for each person served without regard for the actual number of times service will be required or rendered during a given period. It is the most common method of payment to HMOs.

case management   An inter-agency process coordinating a number of services needed by individual patients. It attempts to develop a goal-oriented care plan based on total needs.

closed panel (staff model)   An arrangement where an HMO employs providers and another health-care professionals on a full-time basis. (They may also be employed by an organization that contracts with the HMO.) Sometimes called an exclusive provider organization (EPO).

community rating   A method by which HMOs determine premiums for a particular service area as required by federal law.

concurrent review   This process includes certification for continued hospital stay and screening of bills to avoid duplication that might occur in comanaged postsurgical care.

copayment   Payments made by patients, such as deductible and coinsurance, to discourage excess utilization and help finance benefit programs.

Current Physicians Terminology (CPT)   The basic language of medical claims converting standard terms to code numbers.

deductible   The amount of out-of-pocket expense that must be paid for eye-care service by the insured patient before becoming payable by the carrier.

dispensing fee   The amount paid by an HMO to a pharmacy (and occasionally ophthalmic dispenser) for filling a prescription.

diagnostic related groups (DRG)   A method of controlling Medicare costs by grouping certain services, including the length of hospital stay, into a "package."

diagnostic cost group (DCG)   Developed for Medicare patients covered by HMOs; reimbursement is based on hospitalization patterns for the previous 12 months.

experience rating   The process of determining the premium rate for group risk, wholly or partially, on the basis of group experience.

fee for service   Method of billing for health- or eye-care services under which the provider charges separately for each service rendered.

flexcare   A program that allows employees to designate a portion of their pre-tax wages to pay for add-ons to their existing health-care coverage. This can include dental benefits, eye care, or even nursery charges.

formulary   A list of all prescription drugs approved by an HMO, assembled to promote use of generics.

gate keeper   An agency or process that administers health- and eye-care services provided to an individual or group.

health maintenance organization (HMO)   A prepaid group practice that provides a predetermined benefit package. An HMO can be sponsored by the government, medical schools, hospitals, employers, labor unions, consumer groups, insurance companies, or hospital medical plans. HMOs are both insurers and providers of eye care.

Healthcare Procedure Coding System (HCPS)   The classification system that is used by Medicare. It is based upon CPT but adds additional codes for reporting ophthalmic materials and other items not included in CPT but covered by Medicare.

indemnity plan   In this plan there is a specific payment for designated services. This can go to the enrolled patient or, by assignment, directly to the eye-care provider.

individual practice association (IPA)   IPAs differ from HMOs in that patients go to the offices of member doctors, who are paid on a reduced fee-for-service basis. The IPA concept allows member doctors to maintain the independence of private practice.

International Classification of Disease (ICD)   The codes for classification of conditions used to explain treatment procedures on claim forms.

limited service health care organization (LSHO)   An LSHO is similar to a PPO but organized around a single specialty or type of service.

managed care   A catch-all term that seems to include some aspect of several plans. It involves the control or utilization of quality and claims by using a variety of cost-containment methods. The primary goal is effective delivery.

member services   A department mandated by government regulation to track and resolve any complaints members may have against HMO physicians.

"open-ended" HMO   In this plan members have a choice of two or three gate-keeper providers rather than the usual single gate keeper.

open panel (group model)   An arrangement where an HMO contracts with doctors who have existing practices to provide services in the doctor's own office.

patient assessment categories (PAC)   This may best be described as an attempt to extend Medicare DRGs into the private sector.

peer review groups   Third-party reviewers comprised of local providers who help solve claim disputes and promote fair and ethical practices in the community.

point-of-service preferred provider organization (PSPPO)   See PPO.

preferred provider organization (PPO)   PPOs come in an endless variety of forms. Typically, all have some kind of discounted fee arrangements, put providers at risk, and steer patients to its closed-panel providers either through financial incentives or rules. The PPO model will be the basis for most managed care systems in the near future.

premium   The amount charged by an insurance company for the guaranteed payment of specific benefits.

prepaid programs   Any system that finances the cost of care in advance of services received.

prior approval   Authorization that is required before care can be rendered.

pro-competition   Another cost-cutting device that identifies more efficient and conservative providers and furnishes incentives for patients to choose these doctors.

prospective review   A process that requires the granting of authorization for payment before medical care is provided.

quality assurance   One or more doctors subjectively reviewing work by a peer.

risk management A scientific analysis in which insurance is viewed as only one of several approaches for dealing with risks.

second opinion An additional approval needed by a patient from a doctor who is not financially connected with the organization or person who will be performing the procedure. This information is most often sought in surgical and alcohol-abuse situations.

service area The geographical area from which a particular health-care program draws the majority of its users.

stop-loss A type of insurance purchased by HMOs or providers that limits their liability.

table of allowances A list of covered services that assigns to each a sum representing the total obligation of the plan, but does not necessarily represent a provider's full fee for that service. This is sometimes called a schedule of benefits.

triple option This allows members to choose from HMO, PPO, and indemnity plans.

When Your Patient Enrolls in an HMO

HMOs are enrolling a substantial portion of the population, and competition is a very real fact of life for those of us in the fee-for-service market. Many complain about the unfair economic advantages the HMOs enjoy and express concern about the quality of care provided. HMOs have been referred to as the "K-Mart of health care," and HMO members have been compared to shoppers at discount variety stores. These references imply that quality is not an issue for HMO members; it is only cost that matters.

In any business, however, the three major ingredients for success are quality, cost, and *service*. The product has to be good; it has to be competitive; and one has to provide it in a manner that is satisfactory to and meets the needs of the consumer.

For years, physicians in the fee-for-service market, and optometrists in general, have acknowledged that HMOs provide lower-cost health care but claimed that the quality of care was inferior. This complaint has been levied against closed-panel HMOs in particular.

It's Not as Bad as You've Heard

One study reported that the quality-of-care issue might just be a red herring. The study concluded that HMO doctors simply practice in a different style and it is unlikely there can be large deleterious health effects from their style of medicine.

In general, these plans are very efficient at delivering no-frills quality eye care. Given the fact that about 20 million people belong to HMOs, it is unrealistic to dismiss these groups as purveyors of inferior-quality, discount-variety procedures. Clearly, the place to attack HMOs is the area in which they are most vulnerable — service!

The types of complaints most often levied against HMOs are basically emotional issues. Long waits to get and make an appointment, "gate-keeper" referral mechanisms, restrictions on choosing providers, rude employees, crowded or uncomfortable facilities, and the like seem to result in most of the dissatisfaction.

Your Best Defense

Your advantage as a practitioner in private practice is that you can provide high-quality service for your patients. You don't have to operate within a large impersonal bureaucracy where you have no control over the receptionist's manners or the reading material in your reception room. If you want to improve your practice, think about what constitutes really good service.

Access is probably the most critical ingredient. Keep office hours that are tailored to the needs and schedules of your patients. It is not easy for a person to take time off from work for an eye-care appointment, and one of the biggest advantages of HMOs (particularly the closed-panel variety) is that they provide after-hours care.

Comfort is important to patients as well. Make sure that your office is a pleasant place. Spend some time in your reception and examination rooms. Would it bother you to sit there for half an hour? We've talked about this elsewhere, so I won't belabor the point.

A major feature HMOs offer is their "no-hassle" payment system. Patients don't have to worry about deductibles, claim forms, and keeping track of different payments. While you obviously can't provide the same type of easy-pay service, you *can* handle paperwork and minimize the hassles of dealing with third-party payers.

As prepaid health plans continue to grow and expand, optometrists in private practice need to find the mechanism to compete effectively. Dismissing the competition as "K-Marts of health care" is a futile gesture. In a time when cost-effectiveness carries a tremendous amount of weight, providing top-flight service may easily be the best way to meet and beat the competition. You can't go wrong taking better care of patients.

An HMO in Your Future

And, if you really can't lick them, you can always join them. Managed care plans are here to stay. They will continue to change, as they have been doing for more than 40 years, but as a group, they will also continue to grow.

While developers continue seeking ways to best organize these monsters, remember that nothing is all bad, and some have features that may be advantageous to you. The newest trend is self-funded employer plans. These programs are growing rapidly, but federal law, unfortunately, allows them to discriminate against optometrists. At this point, there are very few new eye-care insurance plans, and these are not being government funded. While the growth of HMOs as a group has slowed, some HMOs are expanding by developing Medicare supplemental programs. Overall, managed care plans are a continuing trend. Take them seriously, but exercise caution when thinking about becoming part of a panel.

A Quick Look at PPOs

To put the whole matter in perspective, I should start by pointing out that 32% of the optometric examinations performed in this country are at least partly covered by an employer, according to the AOA. Rural practitioners might want to challenge that figure, but even if it were halved, there is no way it can be ignored.

The neverending demand for low-cost benefits has contributed to the growth of preferred provider organizations as a cost-effective means of managed care. There are even a number of single-benefit PPOs that offer vision service only through a provider network. The optometrists involved usually contract with insurance companies and employers anxious to add vision to their array of benefit options.

The number of PPOs offering vision care is relatively small, because it is considered an allied health service as opposed to a core benefit. Allied services tend to be optional kinds of coverage, added by the plan's operators only if they have to.

The AOA, of course, takes a more positive view regarding PPOs. Its official position more or less holds that optometry is more efficient than ophthalmology, so O.D.s should be the gate keepers in any eye-care system.

Chain Reaction

And how have the "big boys" responded? No two alike! Some say they accept third-party payment or participate in a prepaid plan, PPO, HMO, or IPA. Others simply offer a discount to qualified groups. Some chains provide eye exams under their programs, others only glasses, and a few offer several alternative plans. A small minority of major retailers have formalized their managed-care marketing to the degree that they sustain a steady sales effort, offering vision-care "products" or service packages to employers, medical insurers, and HMOs. A few say they have decided to forego managed care for the most part in favor of seeking growth in other areas.

There are, however, a few chains that have worked hard enough and long enough to master the intricacies of the managed vision-care marketplace and established full-scope ongoing programs that they actively promote. Pearle Vision and Cole Vision are probably the best examples of chains that take this approach. Each has amassed a sizeable degree of knowledge about the group health-care market. Pearle has actually organized its managed-care offerings into three discreet service packages aimed at different clientele groups, and it has worked out a suitable method for providing eye examinations through its affiliated and franchised optometrists.

Should You Participate?

Let's lump them all together for a moment—vision-care plans, insurance panels, PPOs, Medicare. They have some common pros and cons.

Why Participate?

1. *More patients.* So what if I am busier, but making less money? You'll have to answer that one for yourself. Although every practice is different, there is a lot to be said for volume. The name of your practice will be publicized. Your reception room will be full during periods that might otherwise be quiet. People who come to your office, and are properly impressed, will tell their friends. Some people will even be impressed because their employer or the federal government has recommended *you.*
2. *Improved cash flow.* If your office is on a shaky cash basis, you will be delighted by the speed of most third-party reimbursements. If you have an office computer, you may be able to send your claims over a toll-free telephone line and receive reimbursement within a few days.
3. *Providing full service.* The "we will take care of everything for you" approach appeals to patients. Even if grandmother on Medicare is the only one who will need it, a full-service office is appreciated by the whole family.
4. *Don't ask for cash.* You avoid the uncomfortably competitive position of requiring a large copayment (or full payment) that would be required in another office.

Why Not?

1. *Reimbursement.* There is no such thing as a free lunch. The trade-off in the plan is obviously less money for your professional time. There are plenty of people willing to pay extra for your service if they perceive it to be desirable.
2. *Reduced paperwork and red tape.* If you don't accept assignment, your patients will fill out and submit claim forms, saving you from the task. And, if there is a problem with the claim, it's the patient's responsibility to resolve it. Not a great way to make friends, but it certainly is an advantage.
3. *A better class of people.* The price-oriented seem to come out of the woodwork once your name appears on the list. Not all of them are undesirable, to be sure, but having your name there will bring in persons you'll wish you'd never seen. It happens!

□ □ □ □ □ Six Things You Should Know Before Joining a Third-Party Plan

1. *Be prepared for increased patient volume.* If your third-party plan pays enough for only half your net, you must see twice as many patients just to break even. If you want to get ahead, you will need to see three times as many.
2. *Be ready for a long-term commitment.* You can't just sign up until you "get busy" and drop out. It doesn't work that way. By then you will have already established your mode of practice.
3. *Recognize the limitations.* Contact lenses are rarely covered. Get used to explaining why you must make an extra charge. Upscale frames and lens coatings also are frequently excluded. This might even mean a cash outlay if you have to purchase a substantial stock of inexpensive frames.
4. *Watch out for the medical "gate keeper."* Under some plans, patients are required to see a primary care doctor first. With fellow M.D.s on the referral list, where do you suppose most of the patients will be sent?
5. *Problems with Medicaid patients.* The cancellation/no-show rate of Medicaid patients can be as high as 40%. Many O.D.s automatically overbook.
6. *Watch the details.* Even the smallest mistake can result in a form being returned to you. Delayed reimbursement is expensive.

Getting Paid

"Lower and slower" may well describe third-party fees. We'll talk about using your computer to speed up the process and cut through paperwork in Chapter 13. Software can help ensure correct billing, while automatically calculating the percentage you will be paid. If you are still doing it manually, "super bills" are commercially available.

The super bill sold by HMI (Hays Marketing, Inc.), for example, was designed by optometrist Terry Bonds and will maximize the charges covered by most medical insurance carriers. The reason is simple, insurance carriers train their employees to reject fee slips containing charges for non-aphakic materials and "opias" because refractive diagnosis and prescriptions are not typically covered under major medical plans, including Medicare. Super bills can be customized with your name, address, and HCFA number.

Remember that the basis for reimbursement under the medical model (as opposed to the traditional vision model) is the office visit and additional ancilliary tests or treatments. An office visit should always be charged to capture the cost of basic overhead, staff, sophisticated instrumentation, and the doctor's human capital contribution, in addition to risks involved. The language of medical claims is made up of the Current Physician's Terminology (CPT), the International Classification of Disease (ICD), and the Healthcare Procedural Coding System (HCPS).

CPT is used to report procedures, and ICD is used for diagnoses and symptoms. HCPS is used by Medicare and is based upon CPT, but adds additional codes for reporting ophthalmic materials and other items not included in CPT but covered by Medicare.

Just as judgment must be used in selecting a treatment regimen for a patient, it must be applied in selecting codes to describe them. Thorough documentation of care in each patient's record, coupled with good-faith efforts to code procedures accurately, will result in prompt payment and keep you out of trouble at audit time.

13

□ □ □
□ □ □
□ □ □

Computers in Optometric Practice

W.E. FLEISCHMAN

The path that your practice takes is determined by a series of management decisions. In-office computer systems can have a direct bearing on how well those decisions are implemented. Low-priced computers (PCs), increasingly sophisticated with easier-to-use software, have brought this powerful tool within easy reach of the modern-day optometric practice. The decision should not be *if* the practice should be computerized, but *when!* There are compelling advantages in bringing computerized techniques into the everyday activities of a busy practice.

This wondrous machine—device, contraption, contrivance, or whatever you choose to name it—stands positioned and ready to provide the catalyst necessary to implement your most profound practice management objectives. The transition to computerization should be viewed as *evolutionary*, not *revolutionary*. Most people feel intimidated and confused when they make the decision to purchase their first computer. It is true there is a bewildered array of options available, but it is hoped this chapter will guide you through the maze and will provide ample knowledge for you to make intelligent and wise selections.

The inconceivable advancements in the science of computer technology during the past 20 years are nothing short of miraculous. The office desk-top computer system is a management tool that represents a power resource the prudent practitioner must no longer ignore.

□ □ □ □ □ The Ten Most Important Reasons to Computerize

Improved office organization
- financial analysis at fingertips
- inventory control

Efficient third-party billing
- fewer claims returned
- much more rapid payments

More efficient recall
- recall tracking
- automation

Trace business resources
- determine areas of strength and weakness
- individual production detail

Flexibility of service agreements
- customize to patient need
- expand to "niche" situations

Analyze practice demographics
- major age/sex groups
- percent contact vs spectacle patterns
- define geographical regions (by zip code)

Target mailings
- specific pathological conditions
- new product availability
- bulk-mail savings

Improved billing procedures
- establish audit trails
- trace delinquencies

Expand communications
- patient
- professional
- in-office memos

Economic windfall
- improved staff efficiency
- improved cash flow
- increased patient flow

History

Human beings have always needed to count. The computer is simply another tool to reduce labor and extend the mastery of our environment. Mankind has devised a way to translate an assortment of data and information from the real world into the zeros and ones of the binary code—the language of the computer. The secret is how the computer manipulates these data, encoded as series of zeros and ones of the binary code, with *lightning speed and precision.*

Abacus

The embryonic beginning of the computer was actually the development of the abacus over 1500 years ago. This arrangement of beads and rods was used by merchants for counting and calculating. The device is so efficient and convenient that in some lands it is still in use today.

Evolution

Large-scale electronic computers made their entry in the early 1940s, using vacuum tubes as switching devices and magnetic media for data storage. The internal language that governed early computers was based on the decimal system; virtually every computer since the 1950s has employed the binary system. With only two symbols, the binary system makes for very efficient and much less costly circuitry. The two-symbol approach to expressing information (i.e., the binary code) is accepted as the computer's natural language.

Data Storage and Transfer

Floppy Drives

Magnetic-disk drives are an inexpensive means of storing vast quantities of information that can be quickly retrieved. Standard types are the familiar 5¼-inch floppy disks and the prevailing 3½-inch "floppies," made useful in the popular lap-top portable computers. Now, every system that IBM sells, and many other manufacturers as well, comes standard with the 3½-inch drives.

Hard-Disk System

A hard-disk system (sometimes referred to as a Winchester disk) functions in much the same way as a floppy-disk system, except that the disk is a rigid platter coated with a magnetic substance. It is capable of storing considerably more data than currently available floppy disks. The retrieval of data from the hard disk is approximately ten times faster than from a floppy diskette, which is another important advantage of hard-disk technology. In general, the hard disk resides within the system enclosure in a dust-free environment.

Laser and Optical Storage

Despite the fact that magnetic media are the most commonplace devices for data storage, the entry of laser and optical read-write devices have become more and more apparent. IBM now has a magnetic-optical system (read-write capability) on removable 3½-inch floppy disks. These so-called "floptical" drives and disks have the potential for being the fastest growing storage product since the introduction of the hard disk. However, the magnetic drives will continue to be faster and less expensive in the immediate future. The tantalizing aspect of the floptical disk is its storage capacity, alluded to be 50 to 80 times greater than the current 3½-inch floppy.

Putting It All Together

Although the terminology may seem foreign at first, and a computer's capabilities beyond imagination, you should be reassured that the process of computerization of the optometric practice is not an awesome and unpleasant task. In fact, such an event can be inspiring. The very act of upgrading the practice with such a powerful tool is stimulating.

Streaming Tape Drive

A good, reliable, accurate, and fast backup system is important when you are using any storage device larger than 20MB. The device that fits these criteria is the *streaming tape drive*. Remember that the data is probably worth much more than the physical hardware itself and, often, is simply *irreplaceable*. To provide the basic functionality of such a system, the type of format (medium) used should be a "DC-600" drive. Currently, this drive will store 60MB, 125MB, or 150MB depending on the format used and the tape quality. The hardware interface, a necessary component for the tape drive, should be SSCI (Small Systems Computer Interface), and the software recommended is SYTOS (Sytron Tape Operating System). Qualities essential to the backup device are (1) image backup, (2) file-by-file backup, and (3) verification of the backup data.

It is recommended that the tape backup unit be physically located *externally* as opposed to residing within the chassis of the computer. An external tape drive has its own power supply and puts much less strain on the basic computer system. The external tape drive also allows the convenience of portability so that with proper (and inexpensive) interfaces the unit can be used with other computer systems. It cannot be asserted vigorously enough the need for discipline in the routine of accurate daily backup of the entire database. The recommended system is capable of achieving the speedy backup rate of 5MB per minute in actual use. Once the backup is completed, the tape cassette should be taken off-site, so that in the event catastrophe should strike in the form of fire, theft, or vandalism, the precious data would be safeguarded. In actual practice, it is suggested that two or possibly three tapes be rotated on a daily basis. In this way, if restoring is necessary and one of the tapes has been damaged, at least a second (or third) tape is available with near-current information.

FCC Class B Rating

The FCC class B rating is a legal requirement for the homebound computer, but it is also valuable for systems that will be used only in the office environment. This FCC requirement means the system is less likely to send out unwanted emissions that might interfere with other electronic devices, and it is a much more rigorous and restrictive rating than the FCC class A rating used for business computers. A machine with a class B FCC rating is also better protected from outside interference, as well. For these reasons, you should receive assurance that the computer system you purchase has this desirable class B rating.

Software Considerations

Software applies to those things that cannot be physically touched yet are, in themselves, complete creations. One might think in terms of the music recorded on an audio compact disk (CD). Like the CD, software needs some form of hardware to provide it with an opportunity to have an effect.

Definition

An "application" software program is simply an ordered number of instructions that, when executed in the proper sequence and given the correct data in the proper order and at the right time, yields the desired result. It is wise to keep in mind that computers are best viewed as "idiot servants." A computer—hardware and software—will only do what it is told. Every instruction must be spelled out in great detail, and it must be presented in a way that the computer understands.

The problem with computers is not that they are complicated, but rather that they are very simple—everything has to be explained. A common saying in the computer field is "garbage in, garbage out." That is why it is imperative that building the patient database be performed in a precise and fastidious fashion.

Optometric Practice Management
Application Software

Because there are not many Macintosh optometric practice management software programs in the marketplace, and because the majority of optometric practices seems to be operating under the IBM and IBM-compatible environment, our discussion will be restricted to those software programs designed for IBM (and IBM-compatible) systems.

□ □ □ □ □ **Basic Prerequisites for a Software Package**

The following represents the absolute minimum capabilities of a software package under consideration for installation in the system workstation:

1. MS-DOS compatibility
2. the ability to rapidly and easily back up and restore all data and program files
3. programs for third-party billing (e.g. HCFA 1500 forms)
4. accommodate three or four terminals in a (future) network-type system
5. open item billing
6. ease and proficiency to accomplish data sorts for target mailings, customized recalls, and demographics

The software program must be complete and have capabilities that might not be implemented immediately, but available for use in the not-to-distant future as the office moves in the direction of full computerization. This is not to say a "paperless" office is the hypothetical goal. For the foreseeable future, a paperless office environment is not practical. Written patient records, photographs, and drawings will be needed to bypass the computer system completely.

The Role of the American Optometric
Association and State Associations

The choice of which specific optometric practice management software to use can be perplexing given the number of programs being made available, each with its own features and methodology. It is encouraging that our American Optometric Association has formed a computer utilization committee to research and promote the use of computers among the membership. We have seen a similar effort on a statewide basis in Florida and Kentucky. After a comprehensive review and evaluation, each of these two state organizations elected to take the unprecedented step of endorsing a specific system. Independently, these state associations selected the same system: Crystal Clear Optometric Management by Kellner System of Santa Clara, California (408-986-0383).

Turnkey Systems

Many, if not most, of the numerous vendors of optometric practice management software have available "turnkey" packages that provide both the hardware and software for a computer system. In many instances, the purchase of such a "package" proves to be an efficient and cost-effective approach to the computerization process. However, the selection of the hardware provided with the packaged turnkey system can certainly be tailored to the buyer's requirements, needs, and options. Thus, you need to understand the assortment of hardware combinations available and the attributes of each component to customize your particular practice environment. Such working knowledge creates an efficient and worthwhile platform for a meaningful dialogue between optometrist and vendor, with the added advantage of avoiding misunderstandings relative to the capabilities of the total system package.

□ □ □ □ □ Ten Important Uses for Optometric Computer Programs

Automated recall
- probably the most visible immediate benefit
- reduced staff time and a consistent revenue enhancer
- provides effective method to easily monitor recall compliance
- provides opportunity to customize and target specific ophthalmic conditions

Third-party billing
- ability to respond to consistent pressure from third-party groups, specifically Medicare
- submit claims on computer generated "hard copy"
- capability to submit claims electronically via modem
- priority treatment by provider resulting in faster turnaround and payment

Effective electronic billing
- convenient walk-out statements
- regular monthly billing
- efficient follow-up of delinquent accounts

Service agreements
- print in-office applications

- contact lens replacement
- solutions refill
- planned replacement programs
- eyeglass warranties

Evaluate practice income and growth
- revenue generated from contact lenses or special procedures
- track number and source of referrals
- graph general or specific growth patterns
- daily production reports
- new/returning patients

Monthly, quarterly, year-end processing
- production reports
- recall statistics
- service agreements
- accounts receivable aging

Batch correspondence
- welcome/thank you
- new patient referral letters
- professional referral letters
- appointment confirmation

Marketing
- newsletters
- patient notices
- new product announcements
- patient reactivation program

Laboratory tracking
- by vendor/purchase order
- by date

Inventory management
- bar code
- contact lenses and consignment
- spectacle lenses
- solutions and supplies

Installation and Support

More often than not, there will be some significant amount of anxiety among the office staff regarding the move to computerization; however, much of this apprehension will evaporate with proper indoctrination before and during the time of installation. In general, the installing vendor will arrange suitable training sessions for the doctor and key office personnel prior to and during the installation and follow-up support via an 800 number or telecommunication with the vendor's computer (modem).

Database Installation

We recommend that the initial keyboarding of the patient database be accomplished using a professional and skilled typist employed from a temporary employment service, working after hours when the office is not absorbed in the day-to-events of a busy practice. This will have the advantage of reduced pressure and strain on the office staff as well as avoiding interruption during the normal routine of office activities. This will also ensure that the database is *accurate* and *viable*.

Ergonomic Considerations

Physical Placement of the Computer System

You should plan well in advance for the future location of the major components — central processing unit (CPU), video monitor, keyboard, and printer(s).

A suitable storage area should be selected for the (intact!) shipping containers for future use in the event that it is ever necessary to ship or transport the computer or peripheral devices.

The CPU

The computer itself does not have to be positioned horizontally on a desktop. Inexpensive floor stands are available that allow the unit to be placed beneath a desk or counter; however, cable length and routing may be a limiting factor.

Be forewarned, once the system is "up and running," changing the orientation from vertical to horizontal (or vice versa) may cause erratic behavior of the internal hard-disk drive's read-write head. If such a change is mandatory, the hard disk should be reformatted after being relocated.

Keyboard Placement

Staff considerations in the placement of the keyboard are of primary concern relative to the ease of access, suitable height, and operator comfort.

Give your staff control. The flexible furnishings available to support a computer's components are adaptable and genuinely user friendly, so let your employees have some options when you redesign the office.

A compromise between the traditional typing and desk heights is effective in offering a multipurpose work area for people and equipment. Consider work surfaces that are 28 inches high.

The keyboard connecting cable (with the CPU) is generally limited to about 4 feet; however, cable extensions are available and do not adversely effect the electronic data input.

Your staff should be regulated to avoid partaking of food and fluids (coffee, coke, etc.) in the region of the keyboard. The electronics embedded in the keyboard are easily damaged by dirt, dust, cigarette ashes, and, especially, spilled fluids. Cleaning fluids and/or aerosol sprays are also not recommended on the keyboard.

If a mouse pointing device is to be used *(highly recommended)*, a small clear area must be provided over which to roll it — 10 to 12 inches is adequate. Track balls operate in a similar fashion to the mouse and require less space. Often, these are attached to the keyboard.

Video Display Monitor

Consider *systems furniture.* The interchangeability of parts will give you the opportunity to grow and adapt in the future and will provide variability in monitor location. Electronic considerations limit the connecting cable to a maximum of 4 feet.

Adequate air circulation for proper cooling, about 12 inches, is necessary to avoid harmful overheating and subsequent breakdown and loss of important data.

Placement of the *monitor* with respect for the visual needs of the staff is important:

- Adequate ambient lighting, approximately 50% less than the light from the screen.
- Pay attention to glare. The wrong kind of light can prevent people from doing their best work.
- Use a non-glare screen and/or avoid reflections from overhead lights and windows.
- Consider screen brightness, resolution, and color. Color monitors with brightly highlighted input regions reduce fatigue and errors.
- Don't skimp on chairs. Your employees will appreciate the comfort, and you may even avoid a benefit claim for sore backs.

Printers

The location of the printer is restricted by the electronic constraints of the connecting cable.

Parallel cable (data transmitted like soldiers marching side-by-side) is most commonly used but is electronically limited to a maximum of 6 feet.

Serial cable (data transmitted like soldiers marching single file) provides an optional method of connecting the printer. This is known as an RS-232 connector.

Using a serial connector cable may require an additional hardware upgrade cost, but creates several major advantages in printer location options. The serial cable is thin and easily routed to a remote location and can be as long as 2000 feet without compromising electronic transfer of data to the printer. By using a serial cable, the printer can be located remotely; allowing more efficient space management in the front office area and the major advantage of noise reduction from (dot matrix, impact) printer operation.

The laser printer is virtually noiseless, fast (six to ten pages per minute), and, more importantly, versatile! Desk-top publishing of brochures and/or newsletters is of major importance as a communication tool to improve patient *bonding* to the practice. The major limitations of the laser printer are that they are more expensive than impact (dot matrix) printers, produce more heat, and cannot strike through to print multi-part forms.

Electrical Power and Cabling

The maze of power and data cables that interconnect the various components and peripheral devices should be "color coded" to avoid possible mismatching and subsequent equipment damage.

An inadequate electrical supply can cause erratic performance and data loss, and a separate, dedicated power circuit in the office is recommended. Irregular voltage with power surges and dips can be a hazard and wreak havoc on your system, software, and database. Under conditions of unreliable and unstable voltage control from the power utility, *uninterruptable* power supplies are the treatment of choice.

Summary

Computers are tools. They are powerful machines that deserve our respect, but not our fear. This chapter has introduced you to as much computerese as you'll ever need in the near term. There's much more. Just as you don't have to learn French to travel in Paris or be a pilot to fly from Los Angeles to Chicago, it is not necessary to learn how a computer works or to write a program in order to use one. As a point of curiosity, it might prove interesting. As a point of practicality, it doesn't matter at all.

It is a proven fact that using computers in the workplace leads to growth because businesses that operate more efficiently tend to grow and prosper. Coping with computers is an everyday fact of life; coping successfully is a matter of *survival.*

□ □ □ □ □ Ten Steps to Computerization

Wish list
• Decide what you want the computer system to accomplish.

How big
- Determine patient record base for computer capacity.
- Consider physical area available ("foot print" dimensions).

Who's going to run it?
- Determine staff person(s) responsible.
- Will the vendor educate the staff?

Research software availability
- AOA, local and state associations.
- Colleagues.
- Vendor demonstrations.
- Lease plans and software license plans.

Research hardware availability
- Think quality and expandability.
- Is the hardware compatible with different software?
- Consider possible purchase from software vendor (i.e., turnkey system).

Consider service availability (power source, software, hardware, "help screens," 800 phone-assist lines, modem tie to vendor)

Creating the database
- Will you use staff or outside talent?

Set time frames and goals
- Consider recalls first for immediate positive economic gain.

Plan for future expansion
- Will you need additional terminals?
- Can your system be expanded?

Cost planning
- Should you outright purchase, obtain vendor financing, or lease?

□ □ □ □ □ Some Enhancements for the Future

CD-ROM (compact disc read only memory)
- The compact disc has the ability to hold video images, animation, and stero sound.
- This resource defies easy explanation. Its uses include vast database storage with visual and audio effects.
- Can be used for educational programs and in-office training/screening.
- Ability to store 660 metabytes of data on one CD provides a means of distributing large amounts of information from one source.
- The platform is ideal for references such as *The PDR* (Physicians' Desk Reference), *The Merck Manual,* and other professional resources.

Bar coding

- This technology provides the means to control valuable assets and automate both frame and contact lens inventory.
- Accurate, economical, and easy-to-use systems offer promising solutions to many record-keeping duties.
- New technology can place small lasered labels directly on frames and contact lens vials.
- The ophthalmic community has in place and available a bar code system (OPC) through the efforts of the Optical Product Code Council. This 10-digit numeric code is rapidly becoming the standard for the industry.

Pen-based PSc

- Handwritten input as a means of communicating with the computer has a tremendous appeal.
- This technology allows not only handwriting (actually, printing at present) but also accurate sketching or drawing.
- Pen-based systems will be extremely valuable for editing documents, taking notes, and creating short letters or memos.
- The pen-based system is actually a highly portable supplement to the office desk-top computer system.
- Pen-specific applications are ideally suited for chairside data input to small, lightweight penbooks without the intimidation of the classic keyboard clattering away at the patient's side in a distracting manner.

Fax modems

- Fax technology has been available for about 50 years. Now, with improved telephone transmission, the service has become a daily part of the business world.
- With a desk-top computer, a fax modem, and associated software, the benefits of facsimile document delivery are available.
- These devices allow you to send and recycle faxs while you're manipulating data in another program.
- Fax modems automatically detect whether incoming data are fax or data transmissions and performs its functions in the "background."
- The hardware/software fax packages permit you to intercept a current print routine from virtually any application program and send it as a fax document.

□ □ □ □ □ Where to Buy Ophthalmic Software

Alcon Systems
St. Louis, MO
(318) 289-1700
(800) 289-1991

Alpha Bytes Comp Corp
Niagra Falls, NY
(716) 284-2465

Compulink Bus Sys
Westlake Village, CA
(818) 707-0017
(800) 456-4522

Diversified Ophthalmics
Cincinnati, OH
(513) 321-7988

E.A. Crowell & Assoc
Charlotte, NC
(704) 525-6551
(800) 366-4564

Epoch Technologies
San Diego, CA
(619) 455-0135
(800) 382-8232

Far West Systems
Encino, CA
(818) 905-1410

Global Optics, Inc.
Green Bay, Wis
(414) 432-1502
(800) 289-5367
Macintosh

Harris Comp Sys
Timonium, MD
(301) 561-8130
(800) 368-7797

JEC Software
New York, NY
(212) 786-1962

The M.S. Group, Inc
Davie, FL
(305) 370-4888
(800) 873-1525

Medical Software, Inc.
Waseca, MN
(507) 835-7677
Macintosh

OfficeMate Software Sys
Irvine, CA
(714) 727-7080

OptiMation, Inc.
Northfield, IL
(708) 501) 4434

Optisoft, Inc.
Sandy, UT
(801) 566-6811
(800) 345-7019

Professional Practice Sys
Tacoma, WA
(206) 531-8944
(800) 255-6786

Professional Insight Comp
Garland, TX
(214) 840-3346

Research Computing Sys
Columbia, SC
(405) 341-4339

Richware, Inc.
Tigard, OR
(716) 586-5170
(800) 553-8238

Rivers Computer
Rochester, NY
(716) 586-5170
(800) 553-8238

RLI Corp
Peoria, IL
(309) 692-1000
(800) 331-4930

Systech Systems
Boca Raton, FL
(407) 479-3812
(800) 821-4493

T&M Systems
Kansas City, MO
(816) 455-2428
(800) 729-BYTE
Macintosh

Top Network Info Sys
Mesquite, Tx
(214) 285-8881
(800) 776-8676

Westland Medical Sys
Calabasas, CA
(818) 992-0081
(800) 235-4004

Wibben, Inc.
Gilbert, AZ
(602) 926-4364

William Fleischman, O.D., F.A.A.O.

Dr. Fleischman received his O.D. and M.S. degrees from the University of California, Berkeley, and practiced in Anaheim, CA, before his retirement. He has served as Chairman of the Cornea and Contact Lens Section of the American Academy of Optometry and was Vice-chairman of the AOA Contact Lens Section. The California Optometric Association named him Optometrist of the Year in 1962 and he was recognized as a distinguished Practitioner in Optometry by the National Academies of Practice. He is internationally known as a lecturer and author on a variety of contact lens related subjects and as a clinical investigator, participated in the evaluation of contact lens products for most U.S. manufacturers.

14 □□□
□□□
□□□
□□□

Getting the Most
Out of Your Profession

In some other chapters we talked about the importance of finding role models. Taking a careful look at the way some other person has achieved the things you'd like to have will usually offer clues toward obtaining them. I had several. One in particular was so incompetent I dare not name him, so let's just talk about his key to success. He was in the corridors (never the lecture hall) during *every* optometric meeting, shaking hands, talking to people, and listening to everyone. He knew what was going on, and everyone knew him.

Show people in your community you're alive. Sure, you may understand that, but why waste time on other O.D.s? Doing something for your profession might even seem old-fashioned and unproductive. Just the same, like scores of dedicated colleagues, I've spent a lot of time at conventions or seminars and am totally convinced that it was well worth the effort. Understanding trends and planning for the future call for being where the action is. With observations that most meetings are dull and dreary, I have no quarrel, but I have rarely attended one from which I didn't leave better informed. There are all kinds of professional organizations and they hold meetings for a variety of reasons.

1. Formally structured associations and societies

National. AOA, American Academy of Optometry, NOA (National Optometric Association), OEPF (Optometric Extension Program Foundation), NERF (National Eye Research Foundation), etc. Activities tend to be large-scale, and except for annual meetings, offer more opportunity for work than play. *(Take courses, exchange ideas, meet suppliers, learn about new products. Develop contacts across the country.)*

Regional. New England Council, Southern Educational Congress of Optometry, Southwest or North Central Congresses, and the like. Most of the activity is confined to one big meeting each year. *(Network, talk about fees* and management techniques. Cut a better deal with your rep's supervisor, who knows?)

State. More meetings, more activities, and lots of committees. *(Look for an associate, buy a practice, help influence a legislator, or write an article for your state journal.)*

Local. Area societies cover all the bases. They come in every conceivable size and format. *(Keep a high profile. Help shape opinion where it will do the most good.)*

2. Clinical discussion groups

Not usually well organized but characterized by a hard core of regular attendees interested in some optometric specialty. *(Learn to be a better doctor. Earn the goodwill and kind words of your colleagues.)*

3. Management organizations

Also loosely organized but characterized by intensely interested entrepreneurial optometrists. *(An entirely self-serving activity that can only help your bottom line. You may find a role model here.)*

4. Marketing groups

Usually peers in a specific locality joined for the common purpose of community marketing and recognition. *(Everyone benefits.)*

5. Buying clubs

Although ADO (America's Doctors of Optometry), HMI, and others offer a greater range of services, most members are optometrists with the common interest of quantity purchase to reduce per-unit price of lenses, frames, or anything else. *(Cut the cost of materials.)*

6. Specialty panels

Usually not permanent in nature, these are often established by manufacturers for the purpose of investigating new materials or providing "focus" information. *(All of the above.)*

My advice is to meet with as many as you can. Networking is the name of the game. Most successful optometrists are not loners. Just paying dues isn't enough.

What's in It for Me?

Let's suppose you need some piece of information right now, who will you call? If it has to do with contact lens materials, who would it be?

Or third-party payments? Or a source of medications? Or a meeting time and place? Or referral for a specific problem? Who?

Why did you pick *that* person? And by way of answering the question, how come you didn't pick someone you never see at meetings? Drumming up patient referrals may not be the best reason for standing around after a lecture, but it can't hurt.

A lot of other good things might happen. Conversation leads to practical tips in practice management, buying, staffing, charging, and just about anything else. I recall a post-meeting "bull session" where I mentioned an especially troublesome patient. "Don't worry," a colleague advised, "we had to throw him out of our office." Another chimed in, "So did we," and the three of us went home feeling much better about the whole matter.

Starting Your Own Group

The idea certainly wasn't original, although its success and longevity have inspired quite a few others. Twenty years ago I joined 11 other contact lens–oriented optometrists under a rather ostentatious banner: *The American Society of Contact Lens Specialists* (more often called the "Dirty Dozen"). Through good times and bad, we've met twice a year and have never regretted a second of it. And anyone can do it. For really productive networking, give some serious thought to the invitees and start one of your own.

☐ ☐ ☐ ☐ ☐ Characteristics of a Management Group

The rules are simple

- similar interests
- similar practice size
- no two persons from the same area
- complete honesty
- total confidentiality
- no criticism

A typical meeting agenda

- experience with new products
- marketing techniques
- favorite products
- problem products
- income per doctor
- income per employee
- budgeting considerations

- management ideas
- insurance, health, and retirement plans

Like juries, apostles, and tribes of Israel, 12 seems to be a pretty good number. Once you've tried it, you'll look forward to this most rewarding way to exchange ideas.

□ □ □ □ □ A Productive Meeting of a Small Group

1. *Have a clear purpose.* An agenda mailed before the meeting should include items to be discussed with appropriate time allocated.

2. *Select the site.* The success of a meeting is enhanced by comfortable seating, adequate ventilation, proper lighting, good food, and convenient transportation. In addition to the airport, consider a hotel or motel with easy access to freeway ramps for a successful event. Well-known meeting consultant Dr. Milt Grassell advises picking a site that is slightly more elegant than the places your group might normally frequent.

3. *Disseminate background information.* Everyone will be better prepared if they receive copies of pertinent material beforehand. This little extra work makes the meeting run much smoother.

4. *Select the seating arrangement.* Seating has more to do with the success of a meeting than most people suspect. For example, an auditorium or theater-type arrangement, where all the participants face the speaker, limits the meeting to a sort of lecture by an authoritarian chairperson. Seating that permits participants to face each other is preferable, and a conference table works best of all.

5. *Select the chairperson.* The president of your organization does not have to lead each discussion. On the other hand, the individual who takes charge of each meeting segment must be able to motivate, guide, and keep the discussion moving within limits of the agenda.

6. *Generate discussion.* The best way to get people to speak up often involves asking nonthreatening questions that require only a "yes" or "no" answer—"Should we meet again in November?" or "Can we discuss this at some other time?"

The chairperson ought never begin with something like "We all know that the market is flat, now let me tell you what I think is happening." Far better to say, "We all know the market is flat, what do you think is causing this?"

7. *Keep the discussion moving.* The best tactic involves questions, because anything you want to say can be stated as a question and, psychologically speaking, no one can get upset if you use good judgment: "Joe, you said you liked Frank's service agreement. If you had to make a recommendation, would you make any changes? And why?"

8. *Stay on track.* A meeting will bog down when the same thing gets discussed over and over. Try asking "How does your point relate to the topic we're discussing?" or, "Excuse me for interrupting, but are you bringing up something new?" Paraphrasing will allow you to show you understand, so the discussion will move forward.

9. *End on schedule.* Take the initiative. If the meeting doesn't seem to be going anywhere, someone has to make the decision, tactfully: "As you all know, we have to be on the way home in another hour. Can we wrap this up?"

The Greater Benefit

"What's good for General Motors is good for the nation" was the basis for an Al Capp cartoon character who usually repeated, "What's good for Bullmoose is good for *everybody!*" Just another way of saying "All ships rise with the tide." Participation in association activities helps us all by strengthening optometry.

We've talked a great deal about personal gain in the preceeding pages, and that is OK. I've known people, like my father, who were fanatical in their support of our profession and completely selfless. I've known people, too, who did little more than pay their dues and show up once in a while. There is strength in numbers, and we need both kinds. The real losers are those who neither attend nor belong. Let's close by observing that going to meetings can truly be *good for everybody!*

□ □ □
□ □ □
□ □ □

References

Alpern BB. *Reaching women: The way to go in marketing healthcare services.* Ann Arbor, MI: Pluribus Press, 1987.

Ashe HJ. External influences and the declining practice, *Rev Opt*, April 15, 1963.

Bennis W. *On becoming a leader.* Reading, MA: Addison-Wesley, 1989.

Blanchard K, Johnson S. *The one-minute manager.* New York: Morrow, 1982.

Bredell C. *The Koetting touch, problem-oriented practice.* St. Louis: Vision Publications, 1984.

Brooks WT. *High impact public speaking.* New York: Prentice Hall, 1966.

Brothers J. *How to get whatever you want out of life.* New York: Simon and Shuster, 1978.

Caring for the Eyes of America. St. Louis: American Optometric Association, 1991.

Carnegie D. *How to win friends and influence people.* New York: Simon and Shuster, 1936.

Cetron M, Davies O. *American renaissance.* New York: St. Martin Press, 1989.

Collins M, Thompson B, Hearn G. *Clinical interpersonal skill and contact lens patient's motivation, satisfaction, and recall.* American Academy of Optometry, 1989.

Davidson J. *Blow your own horn: How to market yourself and your career.* New York: Amacom, 1987.

Gallup G, Gallup AM. *The great American success story,* Homewood, IL: Dow Jones-Irwin, 1986.

Graves L. How to dress for success (interview with David Schockley). *St. Louis Business Journal*, Jan. 1989.

Heller R. *The super managers.* New York: E.P. Dutton, 1984.

Hill N. *Think and grow rich.* New York: Fawcett, 1987.

Hoffer D. Show your employees how to shine. *Rev Opt* 1990; 7:29–30.

Johnson R. *The achievers.* New York: E.P. Dutton, 1987.

Koetting RA. Do patients really want cheap lenses? *J Am Opt Assoc* 1979; 50(9):1019–20.

Koetting RA. Utilization of paraoptometrics in contact lens practice. *J Am Opt Assoc* 1981; 52(1):39–42.

Koetting RA. A matter of record. *Opt Mgmt* 1983; 19(5):68–78.

Koetting RA. Let your staff do the marketing. *Opt Mgmt* 1990; 9:67–70.

Levoy RP. *The $100,000 practice and how to build it.* New York: Prentice Hall, 1966.

Locke EA, Latham GP. *Goal setting, a motivational technique that works.* New York: Prentice Hall, 1984.

MacKenzie A. *The time trap: The new version of the 20 year classic on time management.* New York: Anacom, 1990.

Malloy J. *Dress for success.* New York: Warner, 1975.

Miles LL. Marketing from the inside out. *Opt Mgmt* 1990; 7:52–78.

Morrison RH. *The greedy bastard's business manual.* Phoenix: Morrison, Butterfield, and Boyle, 1981.

Nanus B. *The leader's edge: The seven keys to leadership in a turbulent world.* Los Angeles: Contemporary Books, 1989.

Nelson RB. *Delegation: The power of letting go.* Glenview, IL: Scott Foresman, 1988.

Nicola, G. New instruments lead to increased services and revenue. *20/20,* 1990; 10:100–102.

Nightengale E. *Lead the field.* Chicago: Nightengale Conant Corp., 1961.

Osgood C. *Osgood on speaking.* New York: William Morrow, 1989.

Peters J. *Thriving on chaos: Handbook for a management revolution.* New York: Alfred A. Knopf, 1987.

Peters TJ, Waterman RH. *In search of excellence.* New York: Harper and Row, 1983.

Ross M, Ross T. *Big marketing ideas for small service businesses: How to successfully advertise, publicize and maximize your business or professional practice.* Homewood, IL: Dow Jones-Irwin, 1990.

Sachs L. Create classified ads that attract the best. *Opt Mgmt* 1989; 12:34–40.

Sewall C, Brown P. *Customers for life.* New York: Doubleday, 1990.

Smith JN. *Sweat Equity.* New York: Simon and Shuster, 1986.

Stein H. How to write a classified ad that works. *Opt Mgmt* 1990; 10:71.

Sullivan G. *Work smart, not hard: Practical advice from experts and celebrities on how to manage your work, your time, and your money.* New York: Simon and Shuster, 1988.

Townsend R. *Further up the organization: How to stop management from stifling people and strangling productivity.* New York: Alfred A. Knopf, 1984.

Trimble VH. *Sam Walton: The story of America's richest man.* New York: Dutton, 1990.

Weed LL. *Medical records, medical education, and patient care.* St. Louis: Mosby-Yearbook Medical Publishers, 1971.

Winston S. *The organized executive.* New York: WW Norton, 1983.

Wolfe DB. Serving the ageless market. McGraw-Hill, 1990.

□ □ □
□ □ □
□ □ □

Recommended Reading

Baldwin RL, Christensen R, Melton JW. *Rx for success.* St. Louis: Vision Publications, 1983.

Bernstein AL, Freiermuth D. *The 191 best practice building strategies for today's physician.* St. Louis: Mosby-Yearbook Medical Publishers, 1988.

Elmstrom G. *Advanced management strategies.* Chicago: Professional Press, 1982.

Freeman DN. *Systems for success.* St. Louis: Epoch Press, 1987.

Lewis D. *Superopticals beware.* Columbus, OH: Anadem, 1991.

Maino J, Maino D, Davidson D. *Computer applications in optometry.* Stoneham, MA: Butterworth-Heinemann, 1989.

Sachs L. *Do it yourself marketing.* New York: Prentice Hall, 1986.